THE
ULTIMATE
GUIDE
FOR
GAY
DADS

Everything You Need to Know About LGBTQ
Parenting But Are (Mostly) Afraid to Ask

ERIC ROSSWOOD

Library of Congress Control Number: 2017951054

Eric Rosswood

The Ultimate Guide For Gay Dads: Everything You Need to Know About LGBTQ Parenting But Are (Mostly) Afraid to Ask

ISBN: (paperback) 978-1-63353-491-9, (ebook) 978-1-63353-488-9

BISAC - FAM006000 FAMILY & RELATIONSHIPS / Alternative Family
   - SOC064000 SOCIAL SCIENCE / LGBT Studies / General

Printed in the United States of America

To my husband, Mat.
07-07-07

PRAISE

"This is the parenting book gay dads have been waiting for! It takes the basic information you'll find in other parenting books and enhances it by including things specific to gay dads, like finding LGBT-friendly pediatricians, legal steps to protect your family, examples for how to answer questions like, "Where's the mother?" and tons of other valuable information gay dads will appreciate. If you're a gay dad, or you're going to be one soon, you'll definitely want to add this timely book to your library."
—**Stan J. Sloan, Chief Executive Officer,** *The Family Equality Council*

"A fantastic resource and an entertaining read of essential things that gay/bisexual men should know before becoming dads together." —**Chaz Harris, Co-Author of** *Promised Land*

"*The Ultimate Guide for Gay Dads* is an informative and practical book that covers a lot of the essential parenting tips! It includes advice from many parenting advocates, including professionals and gay dads who have helped pave the way for future gay dads. Rosswood has created a valuable resource and tool that should be read by all gay men considering parenthood. And for the existing gay dads out there, there are plenty of wonderful tidbits in the book for you too!" —**Dr. Ron Holt, best selling author of** *PRIDE: You Can't Heal if You're Hiding From Yourself*

"The journey to parenthood is not easy for anyone. For same-gender couples, this journey embodies many twists and turns that are not often documented or discussed in traditional parenting guides directed towards heterosexuals. Rosswood has created an invaluable resource for parents that not only covers traditional topics such as changing diapers and childproofing the home but also more nuanced topics, including traveling as a same-gender family, navigating birth certificate details, and deciding what your child will call you. Whether you already have kids, are deep in the process of starting a family, or only beginning your journey, you will find yourself referring to this book over and over again." —**J. B. Blankenship, author of** *The Christmas Truck*

"*The Ultimate Guide for Gay Dads* is a soup-to-nuts guide for gay fathers and covers all the small and large issues germane to two parents who are men. From choosing a baby name to selecting a physician, from changing diapers to bringing the right toys for airplane rides, from what to call each other to answering invasive questions, this book answers so many questions a gay dad might not even realize he has about raising kids, from babies to toddlers, from children to adolescents. Real-life examples are peppered throughout the book and offer more than one way of handling the many challenges that come up for parents, especially gay dads who face their own unique hurdles. This fun and accessible guide takes the anxiety out of becoming a gay dad. Told in the spirit of love and joy, this guide would make any gay man consider becoming a parent." —**Kathleen Archambeau, Author of** *Pride & Joy: LGBTQ Artists, Icons and Everyday Heroes and Climbing the Corporate Ladder in High Heels*

Thank you for reading **The Ultimate Guide for Gay Dads**. Gaining exposure as an independent author relies mostly on word-of-mouth, so if you see the value in this book and think others will benefit from reading it too, please consider leaving a short review online.
Thank you.

Contents

Foreword by
Writer, Director,
and Producer,
Greg Berlanti

Since I was a child I knew for certain three things about the adult life I imagined for myself. Most people would call these things dreams or aspirations and perhaps they were just that, hopes disguised as premonitions. But for what it's worth, I can't name any vision for my own future I've experienced before or since with the same degree of clarity and definitiveness. So here they are:

The first thing I was certain of as a kid growing up in New York was that I would spend my adulthood in California, and more specifically, Los Angeles. It wasn't because I wanted to work in the entertainment business, that dream was not yet hatched. When I was thirteen my family took a trip to Hawaii and we got stuck in Los Angeles for a layover for a few hours. I went exploring and came across a "Welcome To Los Angeles" sign above the down escalator into baggage claim. Though I'd never seen the sign before it looked familiar to me. And for a very brief moment, I wondered what it must be like to live in a city like Los Angeles with the beaches and Hollywood and the sunny days and warm nights. "I'll live here one day," I thought to myself. That was it. The dream remained but the memory of the sign drifted to the recesses of my brain until almost a decade later when I got an internship during college for a talent manager in Los Angeles. Upon my arrival at the airport, I saw the very same sign and that childhood memory flashed back along with the same feeling of familiarity. It is the same feeling I've had each of the hundreds of times I've seen the sign since...although now I just call that feeling "home."

The second thing of which I was one thousand percent sure was that my career would involve writing. I wrote a lot as a kid, acted in plays, built puppets and performed puppet shows, and like most Gen-X nerds made short films with my neighbor's first Betamax camera. Whether it was on a theatrical stage or behind a puppet theatre or with a camera on my shoulder, no profession or hobby has ever made me happier than dreaming up and crafting a story for an audience. However it is a craft that never came easy to me and still doesn't. And though I've gotten older, and those plays and puppet shows have become television shows and films that studios actually pay me to write, creating stories has never ever gotten easier. Like most if not all the writers I know, I find there is still nothing more daunting than sitting down to face a blank page. So why do so many of us torture ourselves by choosing a profession that makes us feel inferior for the majority of the time? I can't speak for the others, but for myself, in very fleeting moments where everything works and the story comes together and communicates emotionally exactly what I was feeling or trying to say, in those moments I feel certain, more certain than ever, that I'm doing what I'm supposed to do for a profession. I feel home.

The third and final thing I knew for sure about being a grown-up was that I would have a family. I didn't know if that meant I would have a partner for life. I was so young when I first imagined it, I didn't even know for sure I was gay. But there was never a moment during the time I wrestled with my own sexuality that I ever doubted my desire or capacity to be a parent. As young as I can remember, I read books to kids at the library, I started babysitting in eighth grade, and I was a camp counselor throughout most of high school. I had a very close-knit and wonderful family of my own. My parents, both by design and by example, taught my sister and me that family are the people that love you first and most. They are the ones you mark your life by, the people with whom you first bond and clash (and we clashed a lot) and who help you forge the person you are meant to become. That feeling of boundless love and support from those closest to you, through life's ups and downs, that feeling I was taught is also called home.

Now as fate would have it, all three of my "premonitions" came true. I now live in Los Angeles as a professional writer. As of February of last year I am a parent to our son, Caleb. None of these three things occurred in the time or the manner that I thought they would. For instance, I became a parent much later than I imagined—in my early forties—which was not conveniently the same time that my eyes went and I started developing new aches and pains that my doctor diagnosed as the incurable disease of "middle age." And for all my surety that I would one day be a parent, I've had nothing but questions ever since I became one. Simple questions like what's the best diaper to use on sensitive skin? Or what's the best formula to buy? Or do any sleep routines really work? And I've had more complex questions too, some of which pertain to being a gay parent, like what will our son call my partner, Robbie, and myself? Which of us will he call Dad? (He calls us both Dada by the way. Babies are much smarter than you are at figuring out what they want to do.) And I wonder almost every day if I'm a good enough parent. Robbie is great at changing diapers, dressing Caleb, putting him to sleep, comforting him, making him laugh, soothing him, etc. And I'm great at…delivering a running commentary while Robbie does those things. I wondered before Caleb came if I would feel inferior or be competitive. A weird thought, but something I've since learned is not uncommon amongst parents of the same sex. It's as simple as, "Will he have a favorite Dad?" As it turns out, Caleb doesn't seem to have a favorite Dad. He has no idea I'm not as good at changing him, in fact he seems to equally despise anyone trying to put a shirt on his head. But I do have a favorite parent, it's Caleb's other father. And when I watch the two of them together cuddling or playing, it's hard to describe how happy it makes me feel, so I'll just say again it is that same feeling of home.

I hope this book helps you with some of the many questions you'll have about your own family, I know it helped us. Wherever you're at on the journey to becoming a parent, best of luck to you. If you're still thinking and dreaming about it, don't give up hope. If you're about to become a parent, why are you reading this book—go get some sleep! And if you already are a Dad or a Mom, congratulations on fulfilling what was no doubt a life's dream of having a family and a home of your own. You are the luckiest person you've ever met. And so is your kid.

Greg Berlanti

Greg Berlanti
Writer, Director, Producer

Introduction

Congratulations! You've decided to become a dad. You'll soon be entering a brand new world filled with fun and exciting adventures. This is a big moment for you and your family, one that will change your life forever.

Now, parenting is a big, life-altering challenge filled with many ups and downs. There's so much involved with caring for children that an enormous number of books have been written on the topic. A quick search for "parenting" on Amazon brings up more than two hundred and thirty thousand results! There are even entire degrees that revolve around child development. All this sounds like a lot to take in, but the good news is that much of parenting is instinct. Believe it or not, you'll probably know exactly what you need to do when you need to do it, and when you're not sure, there will be plenty of support out there to help you along the way: from your parents and doctors, to Google and, yes, even this book.

Now, I know what you may be thinking: "If so much of parenting is instinct, why do I need to read this book?" The answer is simple really. Parenting as a gay dad is different. "But isn't being a 'gay' parent just like being a 'straight' parent?" Well, yes and no. While it's true that gay parents do all the same things that straight parents do (change baby diapers, feed their children, do their laundry, take them to and from school, help them with their homework, read them stories, kiss their boo-boos, tuck them in at night, etc.), there are many situations that are unique to LGBT parents. For example, having to find LGBT-friendly doctors and schools, asking for paternity leave from work when you're not out to your employer, getting both parents' names on your child's birth certificate, and dealing with nosy, prying questions from just about everyone, everywhere.

One huge parenting difference for gay men is that having a kid is like coming out all over again on a daily basis, especially if you have an infant. Was coming out stressful for you? It's about to get more intense, and you will have a child watching your every move and listening to your every word. If you stutter or pause when responding to prying questions about your family, your children may pick up on you being uncomfortable, and they could start feeling like something is wrong about their family unit. So yes, while "straight parenting" and "gay parenting" are the same, being a gay dad is different and has its own set of unique challenges. That's why I decided to write *The Ultimate Guide for Gay Dads: Everything You Need to Know About Parenting But Are (Mostly) Afraid to Ask.*

This book is a direct follow-up to my previous book, *Journey to Same-Sex Parenthood: Firsthand Advice, Tips and Stories from Lesbian and Gay Couples,* which covered adoption, foster care, surrogacy, assisted reproduction, and co-parenting to help LGBT people make the best decision for expanding their own families. If you are looking to have children but haven't yet decided how you want to start your family, I recommend starting with that book first. *The Ultimate Guide for Gay Dads* picks up where that one left off and covers what happens when and after you welcome a child into your home.

While writing *The Ultimate Guide for Gay Dads,* I talked to doctors, educators, lawyers, and other dads to create a comprehensive book that covers the critical things you should know. I believe this is the perfect supplement to all those other parenting books out there, because it fills in the gaps with information specifically for us gay dads and leaves out all of the irrelevant info. You're not going to find information on how to best aim your nipple into your baby's mouth for breastfeeding. That wouldn't help you feed your baby, and you'd probably get hair in his or her mouth anyway. No—this book specifically covers the basics you need to know and includes a few things you might even be afraid to ask.

Whether you're a gay man welcoming a newborn, adopting an older child, or starting a relationship with someone who already has kids, this book is for you. Now take a deep breath and relax, because you've got this. You're going to be an awesome dad.

The Things About Parenthood No One Tells You About

We've all heard it before. The long list of things people tell you will change when you have kids. You won't be able to go out with your friends anymore. You won't ever sleep again. Your life will revolve around diapers, poop, pee, and puke. They either tell you how much your life is going to suck or how awesome it's going to be. Oh, you're going to have such a cute kid. You'll be able to get them cool clothes, wear matching outfits, throw the best birthday parties...blah, blah, blah. When the news gets out that you're going to have kids, it seems like everyone will want to tell you how they think your life is going to change. But the funny thing is that there are a lot of things that happen when you become a dad that no one tells you about. Here's a list of a few things you should probably know:

1. When you have a baby or toddler, you're going to get kicked in the balls...a lot. Seriously, like all the time. You turn into a play structure and will be climbed on, jumped on, body-slammed, head-butted, and more. Not only will your little dangly bits get kicked, but they'll also get punched, elbowed, kneed, and grabbed. Your kids won't know any better. It'll just be an accident when they're trying to play, but it will be an accident that happens over and over again. Other times, your kid may want to crawl into bed with you when they're sick or they've had a nightmare. Good luck keeping their knees, feet, and elbows still while they're sleeping. Maybe you should invest in an athletic cup.

2. The dad bod is real! Yes, guys with kids gain weight too! Researchers at Northwestern University's Feinberg School of Medicine tracked more than ten thousand men over a twenty-year period: they found that dads experienced an average 2.6 percent increase in their BMI ("Body Mass Index," a measurement of body fat based on a person's

weight in relation to their height), while similar men without kids actually slightly lost weight over the same period. For a six-foot-tall man, this worked out to be an average of 4.4 pounds of dad bod, while a similar man without kids lost an average of 1.4 pounds. This gain in weight may be the result of lifestyle changes, such as family becoming a priority over the gym or eating food off your child's plate when they don't finish. You and your partner may find that you like each other better with a little more junk in the trunk and a little more to hold on to, but if you don't want your weight to fluctuate, be conscious of this beforehand so you can make a better effort to stay healthy. Maybe take turns going to the gym while the other watches the children. If you're someone who likes to cook, maybe come up with a menu plan so that you have healthier options available to eat throughout the week. You can also search for "dad workout with baby" on YouTube to get a few exercise ideas. If nothing else, you'll see a bit of eye candy and can pretend you have the ability to lose weight just by watching.

3. Believe it or not, women are not the only ones who go through neurological and hormonal changes. Men actually go through these changes when they become parents too. Research shows that fathers who are more involved with their children experience a dramatic drop in testosterone and an increase in oxytocin, a hormone that acts as a neurotransmitter in the brain and influences social behavior and emotion. The more interaction fathers have with their children (responding to their baby's cries, playing with their kids, etc.) the stronger the effect. So it you find yourself questioning your sanity after listening to a sappy Top 40 pop ballad

and going through an uncontrollable crying spell because your child's whole life is flashing before your eyes and you think they are growing up too fast even though they're only six months old...don't worry. Your emotional breakdown probably won't last very long.

4. You might not feel an emotional bond right away. Some parents feel a massive rush of love when they hold their child for the first time; there's an immediate connection and the bond is instantaneous. Other parents feel absolutely nothing, and that's OK. For some people, the bond grows over time, as more interaction occurs. Don't freak out or feel guilty if you don't feel the immediate love.

5. There's a chance that you're going to get frustrated with the lack of changing tables available in men's restrooms because many places still limit them to women's restrooms only. When there are no changing stations available, dads are forced to change their baby's diapers on other surfaces (such as dirty bathroom floors or counters), and those unsanitary conditions can pose health risks. Plus, limiting these stations to women's restrooms isn't just a burden on male parents. It's also a casual reinforcement of sexism, hinting that it's a woman's responsibility to take care of children. In 2015, Ashton Kutcher famously launched a Change. org petition asking Costco and Target to stop gender stereotyping and to make changing stations available to fathers too. The petition gained over one hundred thousand signatures and resulted in both stores committing to making a change.

6. If you have an infant, you're going to be changing clothes multiple times a day. Not just your baby's

clothes, but yours as well. There's no escaping it. Even if you use a burping cloth during feeding, you're going to get spit-up and vomit everywhere! It'll get on your shirt, your pants, your shoes, in your hair, on your face and arms. Absolutely everywhere. Unless you want to bask in vomit all day, you're going to want to change. I suggest putting your designer clothes in storage for a year so they won't get ruined...that is, if you still fit into them. (See number two, above.)

7. Speaking of "number two"—if you have an infant, poop is going to take over your life in a way you never imagined. It's not just about how many smelly diapers you're going to be changing. You might even monitor how often your baby poops, the consistency, the smell, etc. You'll have poop horror stories like when your baby shits so hard it exits the top of their diaper and shoots all the way up to their shoulder blades. Or maybe your baby's feet touch his or her butt during a diaper change, and poo goes flying all across the room as they rapidly kick their feet. And yes, it's disgusting. No one likes dealing with it or cleaning it up, but you know what? You'll have great stories to tell, and trust me—you'll be dying to tell them.

8. Building blocks, both large and small, will become your mortal enemy. No matter how hard you and your kids try to clean up, by some mystical magical force, chances are that you will probably manage to find a stray one by accidentally stepping on it with your bare feet. And it will hurt like hell. When this moment occurs, your child will hear you and learn the art of stringing multiple cusswords together.

9. Your child learns to react to things by watching how you react to things. Parenting can be stressful, but if you show that you're stressed, chances are your child will mimic that stress. Take the example above, where the baby is kicking poop everywhere during a diaper change. You may be thinking, "Oh my god! It's getting everywhere, all over the walls and I can't stop it! Ahhhhhhh!" Your baby can pick up on the tone of your voice and your body language. If they pick up that you're stressed, they will probably start crying and screaming uncontrollably until you calm down. It's easier said than done, but try to remain calm when your baby is crying. You could try to ignore the chaos by focusing on singing a nursery rhyme or something. Or if poop is still flying around, maybe it's best to keep your mouth closed and hum the song instead so that you don't have to wash your mouth out later.

10. If you have an infant, keep in mind that about 80 percent of must-have baby products are worthless. You don't need a pee blocker, laundry detergent specially made for babies, or different wipes for butts, pacifiers, and boogers. Don't fall for clever marketing that will clutter your house and leave a hole in your wallet. Just stick with the basics. For a full list of recommended baby products and a list of gimmicks you can avoid, see page 70.

11. You will get looks from women every time you go out in public alone with an infant. Some will stand back and stare at you, watching your every move. Some will boldly approach you and ask where the baby's mother is. They may be suspicious, thinking you've kidnapped the child; or they may have admiration for you, thinking you're helping your "wife" by taking the baby out for a bit and doing

the grocery shopping. Some may even feel sorry for you, thinking you need help—because a man can't possibly know how to take care of a baby. I'm not making these reasons up either: they are things women have actually said to me in public when I was out with my infant son. I'm not sure if it's a maternal instinct or what, but I've never had a male react the same way to me. Be prepared for these awkward situations and see page 191 for ideas on how to handle awkward situations and questions from people.

REAL-LIFE STORY:

"When we were out with our kids or another set of gay dads, various women felt absolutely no restriction keeping them from invading our space or addressing our children directly without even making eye contact with us. One time, we were at a restaurant with another gay dad family. A woman at the next table came over and starting making baby noises to my friend's son. She then picked him up without asking and tried to walk him around the restaurant. If the gender roles have been reversed, the cops would have been called."
—Rob Watson

---

12. Tons of people are going to want to give you advice on how to take care of your children, even people who aren't parents. Keep this in mind, though: every child is different, so what works for one kid may not necessarily work for another kid. Even with your own children, what worked for your first child may not work for your second or third. Most of parenting

is trial and error. Trust your instincts. You know your kids best, and you'll figure out what works best for them. Take suggestions if you want to, but don't feel like you have to listen to everything other people say. 90 percent of parenting advice is nonsense, except for what's in this book. This book is filled with fabulous information you can't live without, and even if you don't agree, you can still get some use out of it as a booster seat or doorstop or something. It also makes a great fashion accessory for your morning commute.

Coming Out as a
Gay Parent

Do you remember coming out of the closet? Were you anxious and maybe a bit paranoid? Did it take you a while to get comfortable in your own skin? Well, get ready for all of those emotions to come flooding back. Having a kid is like coming out all over again, on a daily basis—especially if you have an infant. Strangers everywhere, from people in line at the grocery store to those working behind the counter at the dry cleaners, will want to tell you how cute your baby is...and then they'll want to know where his or her mother is. As your child gets older, you'll be coming out to their teachers, coaches, friends, the parents of their friends, and more.

In the beginning, if you have an infant or toddler, you may be able to control the conversation and choose how you'll respond to prying questions from strangers (See page 189). While you're waiting in the checkout line, do you want to go into the whole story about how your child was conceived and/or how your family was created, or do you just want to pay for your groceries and go home? Also, there may be times where you're not sure if the environment you're in is LGBT friendly. If that's the case, maybe you don't want to go into too many details.

When you have a toddler, or an older child who is able to speak, they may even be the ones outing you. They might be jumping up and down with joy to talk about their two dads, and the younger they are, the fewer filters they'll have. I'm not saying that you shouldn't be proud of being a gay dad. To the contrary, I think you should be out, proud, and loud, and we should foster an environment where our children are proud of their families too. All I'm saying is that having a kid is like adding a spotlight to your being gay, and before you just had to worry about yourself. Now you have to think about your little one too, and they'll be watching your every move. If you stutter or pause when responding to prying questions about your family, your children may pick up on you being uncomfortable, and they could start feeling that something is wrong with their family unit. So be ready for it, and practice what you're going to say and do before you get asked the questions. Talk to your family and friends about it too, so they know how to respond when your child is present.

GAY MEN TALKING ABOUT HOW VISIBLE THEY ARE AS DADS

"The three of us going out in public together is like putting a neon sign above our heads that says: GAY DADS. We get the stares; most are welcoming, but we have had a few judgmental glares. It's strange, going from being a couple that would not draw much attention (if any), to being a family that everyone notices. I knew prior to adopting that we would have to be out and proud because we would be more obvious, but I didn't expect it to be as much as it has been. We talked to our family about being proud of who we are because if we act ashamed of our family, our daughter will grow up feeling the same way. I've had a few arguments with my mom for telling her neighbors that I have a wife, and we can't have anyone showing our daughter that our family is less than any other."
—Chad Scanlon

"I'm divorced now, so people just see me and my son together, not two gay dads and a kid. Our son was three years old when we separated, and people don't really ask me prying questions anymore. We're lucky because we live in an accepting community, but I will say, though, airports are where it always got weird. There were lots of stares from people. I'm the type of person who just stares

right back. I literally don't stop until you look away."
—**Frank Lowe**

"At our daughters' former nursery school, we were the only LGBT-headed family. During the second year with the school, I arrived late to an All Parents Meeting. It was standing room only, so I stood in the doorway near the front of the room. Everyone in the meeting was facing in my direction. A new parent had stood to ask the question, 'Have we done outreach to try and diversify attendance? For example, have we reached out to LGBT-parented families?' Every head immediately swung around and looked right at me, standing there at the front of the room. I just slowly raised my hand and, with a sheepish smile, said, 'Um, that would be me?'"
—**Bill Delaney**

"The questions have decreased drastically since Harper has been able to speak in complete sentences, and because she is determined to talk to everyone. She does not grasp the concept of 'stranger danger,' unless you are dressed as the Easter Bunny. We are now 'outed' everywhere we go. Whether we're at the hardware store, our bank, or the TSA line—everyone knows that Harper has two dads. Harper either tells everyone, 'This is my dada and this is my daddy,' or she will quickly correct someone, with sass, if they make a comment about her daddy, and they are talking to Matthew."
—**Trey Darnell**

"Neither of us likes to harp on what we can't change. We are visible. When we go out someplace, we are different and people let us know that—whether they are asking kind but inappropriate questions, or just staring and gawking at us. At some point it will just be. Don't get me wrong, most

everyone is kind to us and genuinely curious."
—Duke Nelson

"As a gay man, I feel I had to learn not to care about what people thought about me. Holding hands in public, a slow dance with my college boyfriend, a kiss in public...I've found that attitude serves me as a dad too. Whether I was changing a diaper in public, walking around in a freshly soiled shirt, or dealing with a tantrum, I feel being gay prepared me to ignore the gazes of strangers."
—Ian Hart

Name-Calling

When straight people have a baby together, it's pretty much assumed that one of them is going to be called mom and the other will be called dad. Or mother and father. Or something else similar, based on societal norms. But what happens when a child has two dads? Can a kid refer to both of his or her parents as dad? The short answer is yes. People can choose whatever names they want for themselves. Chris and Josh may find that using the names "Daddy Chris" and "Daddy Josh" works for them and their family. Other parents may decide they want to assume a more unique name that differentiates them from each other, and that's fine too. It's all going to boil down to personal preference. What do you want to be called? If you haven't decided on a name for yourself yet, here is a list of various synonyms for a male parent.

- Dad
- Dada (Dadda)
- Daddy
- Father
- Poppy
- Pop
- Pops
- Pa
- Papa
- Papi
- Pappy

If you're still having trouble picking a name for yourself, or if you just want to be more creative, here is a list for how the word "dad" is translated in various different languages.

Language	Translation
Afrikaans	Vader; Pa
Albanian	Baba; Atë
Basque	Aita
Bosnian	Otac; Tata
Catalan	Pare
Croatian	Otac; Tata
Czech	Táto; Otec
Danish	Far
Dutch	Vader; Papa

Esperanto	Patro
Estonian	Isa
Filipino	Ama; Tatay; Itay;
Finnish	Isä
French	Papa
Frisian	Heit
Galician	Pai
German	Papa; Vater
Greek	Bampás
Hawaiian	Makuakāne
Hindi	Pita
Hungarian	Apa; Apu; Papa; Edesapa
Icelandic	Pabbi; Faðir
Indonesian	Ayah; Pak
Irish	Athair; Daidí
Italian	Babbo; Papà
Japanese	Otōsan; Papa
Korean	Appa
Latin	Pater
Latvian	Tēvs
Lithuanian	Tévas
Luxembourgish	Papp
Malay	Bapa
Maltese	Missier
Norwegian	Pappa; Far
Polish	Tata; Ojciec
Portuguese	Papai; Pai
Romanian	Tata
Russian	Papa
Samoan	Tama
Scots Gaelic	Athair
Serbian	Tata
Shona	Baba
Slovak	Ocko; Otec

Spanish	Padre; Papá,
Swahili	Baba
Swedish	Pappa
Vietnamese	Cha
Welsh	Tad

The list above is not a full list, but it gives you a good idea of what's out there. If you are curious about more languages, or the pronunciations of any of the words above, Google Translate is a great resource.

DID YOU KNOW?

In a 2005 interview with Rolling Stone, while promoting Star Wars: Episode III - Revenge of the Sith, George Lucas explained that there is a special meaning behind Darth Vader's name. He was quoted as saying, "'Darth' is a variation of dark. And 'Vader' is a variation of father. So it's basically Dark Father. All the names have history, but sometimes I make mistakes—Luke was originally going to be called Luke Starkiller, but then I realized that wasn't appropriate for the character. It was appropriate for Anakin, but not his son. I said, 'Wait, we can't weigh this down too much—he's the one that redeems him.'"

REAL-LIFE STORY:
"We were going to do 'dad' and 'papa,' but that's not what our kids wanted to call us. We adopted our son when he was five years old, and he just started calling me 'daddy' and my husband 'dad'. When we later adopted his sister, she called us by the same names her brother used." –Jay Foxworthy

CHOOSING BABY NAMES

If you've thought about becoming a father, chances are that you've probably had a few baby names floating around inside you head. Maybe you've discussed names with your partner and have jotted them down on a list somewhere. Maybe the perfect name came to you in the middle of the night. Should you go with something unique and cool, or should you stick with something more traditional? If you adopt an older child who already has a name, you don't have to worry about any of this, but if you are adopting a baby from birth, you're going to have to pick a name for your baby, and it might not be as easy as you think.

What If You Don't Get to Choose?

For example, if you are going through open adoption, there's a chance the child's birthmother will want to choose the name because it's something she can provide for her baby. There's a lot to think about in this scenario. If the birthmother wants to name the baby, will you keep the name, or will you legally change it later, perhaps when you finalize the adoption and get an updated birth certificate? Before doing this, think about the impact this will have on your child growing up. Is there a possibility they will think you took a piece of their identity away from them?

Even if the birthmother wants to name the baby, that doesn't necessarily mean you can't be involved. Maybe naming can be a joint effort. Since people typically have three names (first, middle, and last), perhaps the birthmother would be open to choosing the middle name and letting you choose the first and last. There are many possibilities and things to consider.

What about the Last Name?

Speaking of last names, how will you choose one for your baby? If you and your partner have different last names, what will the last name of your baby be? Will he or she take one of your names, and if so, which one? Will the baby take both of your last names, and if so, will you hyphenate them? Which one will be first?

My husband and I never had to consider the last name scenarios because we combined our last names when we got married. My last name used to be Ross and his was Wood. We combined them to Rosswood and our son was given our last name when he was born. We feel that all of us having the same last name strengthens our family unit, but that's just us. You'll have to decide what works best for you and your family.

Teasing with Acronyms

Now, when choosing names for your child, it's important to take many things into consideration in order to limit the chances of them getting teased down the road. For example, what will the initials spell? Ashley Summer Smith would probably be referred to as an ASS, making high school a living hell. Daniel Ivan Kennedy would probably be called a dick; Trevor Ian Thompson would be called a TIT. But it's not just naughty words you have to consider. My name used to be Eric Alan Ross and my initials spelled EAR. Kids in school used to tease me by flapping their ears like Dumbo when talking about me. Also, names on school lists are often put in order by Last, First, Middle initial, so mine was listed as Ross, Eric A. Whenever I had a new teacher, or if there was a substitute, they would call out "Erica" during roll call. Since I was openly gay in school, everyone in class would laugh and use it as an opportunity to make fun of me for being gay. Kids are cruel.

Spelling

There are more than acronyms to take into consideration when it comes to teasing. I'm sure we've all seen the picture of the cake online that was supposed to say "HAPPY BIRTHDAY CLINT," but the letters were too close together so CLINT wound up looking like CUNT. If you haven't seen the picture, just Google "Clint birthday cake." I'm sure Clint was thrilled when he saw it. Best birthday ever.

Rhyming

Just when you think you've found the perfect name, you might want to run it through the rhyming test. If the name can be rhymed with something bad, making your child a target for teasing later in life, you might want to hold off and think about it a bit more. Here are a few examples of names that can turn into rhyming nightmares for your child.

- Cooper the pooper
- Jude the prude or Jude in the nude
- Tucker fucker
- Esther the molester
- Scabby Abby
- Colin colon
- Lucas mucus
- Lydia chlamydia

In the end, it's important to remember that kids will eventually get teased about something in their lives no matter what. Teasing is a fact of life and there's nothing we can do to prevent our kids from ever being teased, but we can raise them to be strong. In the end, if there's a name you're dead set on, it's up to you whether you want to use it.

Shh! It's a Secret.

One last thing when it comes to baby names. Keep in mind that if you mention any of the names you're considering to friends, family members, coworkers, etc., you are inviting people to give you advice, solicited or not. Unless you want it to become a debate, you may want to keep the list of names to yourself.

Taking Time Off Work

Am I Legally Allowed to Take Time off from Work When I Have Children?

According to the United States Department of Labor, at the time of this publication, the Family and Medical Leave Act (FMLA) entitles an eligible employee to take up to twelve workweeks of job-protected unpaid leave when they welcome a new child as part of their family. Some states have similar laws that may apply to more employers than FMLA does. This includes the birth of a baby via surrogacy, both domestic and foreign adoptions, and the placement of a child through foster care. Even though this family leave is unpaid, employers are required to continue employee healthcare coverage during this period.

Your employer may require that you use your saved vacation days and any other paid leave first, but that leave will not count towards your FMLA leave. So, if your employer requires you to take two weeks of paid vacation, you may still take an additional twelve weeks of unpaid FMLA leave (fourteen weeks total: two weeks of paid vacation, plus twelve weeks of unpaid FMLA leave).

Some states also offer some sort of paid family leave. At the time of this publication, only California, New Jersey, New York, Rhode Island, Washington, and the District of Columbia (starting in 2020) require paid family leave—but other states may quickly follow. Some companies have even added paid family leave as an employment benefit to become more competitive, even though the state they are in does not require it. Check with your employer to see what benefits you qualify for.

Can I Be Fired or Demoted for Taking Time off under FMLA?

Technically, your company cannot legally discriminate against you for taking qualified time off under FMLA. They are required to give you back your original job when you return or give you a new position with equivalent pay, benefits, and terms and conditions of employment. However things are not always cut-and-dried.

"More than half the states do not have explicit laws protecting employees from discrimination based on sexual orientation or gender identity," explains Cathy Sakimura, Deputy Director & Family Law Director for the National Center for Lesbian Rights, "although both federal and state anti-discrimination laws prohibiting discrimination based on sex should apply to protect LGBT workers."

So while a company can't technically fire you for taking time off under FMLA, some may try to get away with firing you if they find out you're in a same-sex relationship. If you are not out at work, and/or you fear you might be retaliated against for being LGBT, seek the advice of a lawyer before giving your employer information about your family expansion plans.

What If I Am Not Out at Work?

As mentioned above, over half of the states do not have laws that explicitly protect employees from discrimination based on sexual orientation and gender identity, so not everyone has the luxury of being out at work. If you want to take a leave of absence from your job, talk to a lawyer before telling your employer about your plans. Otherwise, you could always save up your vacation time and take a couple of weeks off instead of FMLA or state family leave, although that won't give you very much time to bond with your child.

Even if you don't plan on taking time off, consider what happens after you welcome a new child into your home. Do you need to add your child to the health insurance you have through work? If so, there's paperwork to fill out and someone in HR will have to process it.

Also, keep in mind that if you tell anyone at work that you are having children, or already have kids, they are probably going to ask you about your "wife" or the "baby mama." This could open up prying questions about your relationship status and your home life. Think long and hard about how you want to respond to these questions and what cans of worms you are comfortable opening.

While not impossible, it may be hard for you to keep it a secret that you have kids after you actually have them. You may need to rush home early to pick them up from school if they get sick, you may need to take time off to take them to doctor appointments, or something else may come up where your kids take precedence.

What Are Some of the Concerns Men Have for Taking Parental Leave?

In 2016, Deloitte and KRC Research conducted a parental leave study with an online poll of one thousand employed adults across America with access to employer benefits. They found that fewer than half of the respondents felt their company fostered an environment in which men were comfortable taking parental leave. While 64 percent of workers surveyed said that companies should offer men and women the same amount of parental leave, 54 percent felt their colleagues would judge a father who took the same amount of parental leave as a mother. The study also found that more than one-third of respondents felt that taking parental leave would jeopardize their position, more than half felt that it would be perceived as a lack of commitment to the job, and 41 percent felt that they would lose opportunities on projects.

In addition to the findings by Deloitte, the Toronto University's Rotman School of Management released a report in 2013 showing that involved fathers were looked down on by their colleagues and treated worse at work than men who stuck closer to "traditional gender norms." There is good news though: more and more men are choosing to take parental leave as more and more companies are offering it as a benefit. It also helps crush stereotypes when executives lead by example. Mark Zuckerberg, CEO of Facebook, made national headlines when he took a leave of two months following the birth of his daughter and Chad Dickerson, former CEO of Etsy, took nine weeks off when he adopted his son. When top executives take family leave, it demonstrates the company's values through actions and not just words.

How Can I Make Taking Time off Work Easier?

Many people fear that taking extended time off from work will be disruptive, so here are a few tips to make things as easy as possible:

1. **Tell Your Company Early** – Make sure you tell your company early so that you can work together to

come up with a transition plan, and so other team members can seamlessly fill in while you're gone.

2. **Be as Transparent as You Think You Can Be** – Births are not always on time, and you may be in a situation where you have to leave at a moment's notice. Or maybe you'll have to fly to another state to meet a birthmother a few months beforehand. Keep your employer aware of such possibilities if you can.

3. **Create a Plan** – Work with your supervisors and peers to come up with a handoff plan so that things will work seamlessly while you're on leave. Make sure everyone on your team knows who is covering what part of your job and whom they should contact if they need help.

4. **Talk to Other Fathers** – If there are other fathers at your company who have taken family leave, don't be afraid to reach out to them and talk to them about their experience. Ask them how it went and whether they have any advice on how to make the experience easier for you.

What Should I Do If I Feel Like I'm Being Discriminated Against?

If you believe that your rights under the FMLA have been violated, you can file a complaint with the Department of Labor by going to www.wagehour.dol.gov. Before doing anything though, you may want to consult with a lawyer. Lambda Legal, the National Center for Lesbian Rights (NCLR), American Civil Liberties Union (ACLU), and GLBT Legal Advocates & Defenders (GLAD) all help fight for LGBT equality in courts and have lists of attorneys who are LGBT friendly. They can provide legal information and contact information for attorneys in your area.

If I Become a Stay-At-Home-Dad, Will It Be Hard for Me to Re-enter the Work Force?

The number of stay-at-home dads has slowly been increasing over the last few decades. According to the Pew Research Center, there were roughly 280,000 men who stayed at home with their kids in the 1970s. That number increased to 550,000 in the first decade of this century. The study analyzed data collected in the Current Population Survey (CPS), conducted by the US Census Bureau and the Bureau of Labor Statistics. The data only included married couples with children where at least one spouse worked a minimum of 35 hours a week—and since the US federal government did not recognize marriage equality until 2015, the study did not take same-sex couples into consideration. The fact still remains the same though. As time goes by, more and more fathers are choosing to stay at home with their kids.

So what is it like for these fathers when they try to re-enter the work force? Unfortunately, many of these men find it difficult to find jobs. There's a stereotype out there that women who stay at home with the kids are caring, while men who choose to do the same thing are putting family over their careers and don't have the drive or dedication needed to fill leadership positions. Hopefully this stereotype will go away as more men choose to be stay-at-home dads—but until then, here are a few steps you can take to make it easier for you to re-enter the work force when you're ready:

1. Stay connected with your industry contacts. They can be references for you down the road.

2. Read articles, take night courses, volunteer, or do anything else that can help keep your skills up-to-date.

3. Keep networking and stay well-informed on the job market in your area.

4. Keep your LinkedIn profile up to date and let your connections know you are looking for work. Ask them whether they know of any job openings, and if they can help you get an interview.

Protecting Your Family

Why Should the Names of Both Parents Be Listed on a Child's Birth Certificate?

So what's the big deal with putting the names of both same-sex parents on a child's birth certificate anyway? Birth certificates are solely for identifying genealogical heritage, right? Wrong! Parents are often required to produce birth certificates to establish parental rights and/or to prove they have the authority to take action on their child's behalf. If a same-sex parent is not listed on their child's birth certificate, it can sometimes prevent them from doing things like authorizing critical medical treatment or performing basic tasks such as enrolling their child in daycare, school, or extracurricular activities. Having both parents' names on a birth certificate can help provide LGBT couples and their children the privacy, dignity, security, support, and protections that are given to married opposite-sex couples and their children.

Can a State Refuse to Put Both of Our Names on Our Child's Birth Certificate?

They used to, but now every state must put both same-sex spouses on their child's birth certificate. Marisa and Terrah Pavan, a legally married lesbian couple living in Arkansas, gave birth to a baby girl in 2015 via an anonymous sperm donor; however, the Arkansas Department of Health refused to issue Marisa's name on the birth certificate and listed Terrah as the only parent. Leigh and Jana Jacobs, another legally married lesbian couple living in Arkansas, were also denied their request to add both of their names to their son's birth certificate when he was born.

At the time, a husband of a married woman was automatically listed as the father even if he was not the genetic parent—but that was not the case for same-sex spouses. So, with the help of the NCLR, the two couples sued for equal rights and won. In June 2017, the US Supreme Court ruled that states must treat married same-sex couples equally when issuing birth certificates and that this equal treatment was required by Obergefell v. Hodges, the 2015 marriage equality case.

"All states put the woman who gives birth on the child's birth certificate," says Sakimura, "unless the state allows surrogacy or there has been an adoption or other court order. This means that two gay dads—or a single gay dad—can be on the birth certificate if they used surrogacy in a state where that is allowed or they adopt."

Does My Name on My Child's Birth Certificate Give Me Full Legal Parental Rights?

Even if you are legally married, and both of your names are on your child's birth certificate, a birth certificate doesn't guarantee you will be protected if your parental rights are challenged in court. Because of this, it's important that all non-biologically related parents protect themselves by doing an adoption, or by getting a court order. If you have an adoption or court order recognizing that you are a parent, the law should treat you and your family like everyone else. If you are unmarried, you need an adoption or court order even more, because most unmarried parents who are not both biological parents cannot be on the birth certificate any other way. If you have any questions about your parental rights, you should consult a family lawyer.

What Else Can I Do to Legally Protect My Family?

Everyone, regardless of their sexual orientation or gender identity, should have a will in place to protect their families. A will should name all beneficiaries and be detailed in listing what you want to happen in the event that you are no longer able to care for your child due to death or injury.

Let's Go Shopping!

Yay! Isn't it great to have an excuse to go shopping? How much fun is it going to be to pick out adorable baby clothes, a decked-out stroller, and a cute, stylish diaper bag that's different from all the others and basically shouts out to everyone, "I'm the coolest, most fashionable daddy in the world"?

Stop right there! Hold on! While you may have mastered going to the mall and picking out fashionable clothes for yourself, navigating a baby store is a whole different monster, filled with gimmicky, money-sucking products around every corner. The packaging tells you that you need this item to keep your baby safe or to make a basic parenting routine easier. Do you really need a bathtub thermometer? How about baby kneepads to protect your child's knees while they're learning how to crawl? Protection is good, right? Check out the lists below to see what kind of products you really need and which ones you can live without.

Must-Have Products for New Babies

Car Seat – This goes without saying. They're required by law every time you drive somewhere with a child in the car, and hospitals won't even let you take your baby home without one. There are three stages of car seats for growing children: rear-facing (for infants), forward-facing, and booster seat. Convertible car seats are also available with the benefit of being specially designed to safely convert from a rear-facing to a forward-facing position.

When purchasing a car seat, make sure you get one that meets the Federal Motor Vehicle Safety Standards (FMVSS), and that you choose the correct seat for your child's age, height, and weight. The manuals for the seats will have the height and weight specifications; this information will most likely be found on the actual seat itself. Infants will need a rear-facing car seat—in fact, the American Academy of Pediatrics recommends that children ride in rear-facing seats for as long as possible.

Diapers – You're going to use a lot of these, so stock up…but not until you're 100 percent sure what size your baby will be wearing. The size of the diaper your baby wears will depend on his or her weight. While you may think a newborn baby will automatically need to wear a newborn-sized diaper, if he or she winds up being born at 10½ pounds, they're going to look like they're wearing a Speedo. It's best to buy a small pack of diapers for the first round, and then stock up once you know for sure what the correct size is.

TIP:
You'll have to buy diapers often, and the boxes can be big and bulky, taking up a lot of space in your car. The box might be difficult to carry back into the house when you're carrying a little one as well. If possible, consider ordering diapers and other big, bulky items online so they are delivered straight to your door.

Wipes – You will need plenty of these during diaper changes, but they're not just for butts! Wipes have many other uses too. You can use them to clean faces, hands, clothes, counters, and many other things. Wipes will become your new best friend. They come in a variety of scents, scent-free, and hypoallergenic versions. Keep stashes in various places around the house (bathrooms,

baby's room, kitchen, etc.) and never leave home
without them.

Baby Clothes – Obviously your baby is going to need
something to wear, but what exactly do you need to buy,
and how many of each item should you get? Be aware
that babies grow fast, so there's a chance that your child
could move up to the next size before they even get an
opportunity to wear what you bought. Think about it. Baby
sizes are 0–3 months, 3–6 months, 6–9 months, and 9–12
months. You're basically buying a whole new wardrobe
every season! That can get expensive quick, so here
are a few tricks to help you avoid needing to take out a
second mortgage:

TIP:
*You may have the urge to buy stylish designer outfits.
Keep in mind that babies grow fast, and you'll wind up
spending a lot of money for something your baby will
only wear a couple of times–maybe even just once!
Unless you want to get a designer outfit for a photo
shoot, consider skipping it to save money.*

1. Keep all your receipts and the tags on the clothes,
   until you're ready for your baby to wear the clothes
   you've bought. Even though you may have the urge
   to wash everything and put them in the dresser right
   away, try not to do this if you can. This way, you
   can return things if your baby grows out of them
   before he or she can wear them.

2. Buy a size up. Babies grow fast, so they'll be able to
   wear those larger-sized outfits in no time.

3. See what the clothes are made out of. The more cotton a piece of clothing has, the more it's going to shrink—so even if you buy the right size, it may not fit after you wash it.

4. Convenience and practicality should come before style, always! This may be one of the most difficult things, but try as hard as you can to resist the urge to buy clothing just because it's cute. Nothing is worse than waking up in the middle of the night to change a poopy diaper while in zombie mode, and then being stuck there with a screaming, squirming baby for what seems like forever because you can't unbutton their clothes. Why spend money on something that you'll never even want to put on your baby because it just frustrates you? At the end of the day, you're not going to care how cute that little sailor outfit is, even though it came with an adorable matching hat and tiny little socks. If it doesn't give you easy access for diaper changes, forget it!

5. Don't forget hand-me-downs. Many people store baby items after their children outgrow them and then give these things to other people in the community who have recently had children. If you know a friend or family member with children slightly older than yours, you might just score a few free toys and/or outfits. Also, consider saving items your child outgrows so you can pay it forward, or so you can have stuff available for your next child if you plan on having more.

Now, as for what clothes you should get, here are a few suggestions:

- It typically takes about two weeks for a baby's umbilical cord to fall off. During those first couple of weeks, it will irritate your baby if anything (like snaps, buttons, or zippers) rubs up against it. Consider getting a few undershirts that open in the front and have snaps on the side, to use until the belly button heals.

- Onesies come in a variety of different styles. Some come with no legs and button up in the crotch. These are great for easy access when changing a diaper, and they don't ride up. Others come with legs, and some even come footed to keep your baby's feet warm without socks. Because onesies with zippers or snaps are easy to get on and off, it'll help keep your sanity if these dominate your baby's wardrobe for the first few months.

- Babies lose a lot of heat through their heads, so you'll want one or two beanie-style hats to keep your baby's head warm.

- Socks are a pain in the butt because they always wind up falling off. Just get a few to start with and see how it goes. Remember, footed onesies also keep feet warm.

- You'll probably need a sweater or hoodie to keep your baby warm while going outside. Look for something that's easy to get on and off and doesn't have drawstrings. If you go outside in the cold a lot, you may need a backup or two for times when the main sweater is in the wash.

> *TIP:*
> *Two-piece outfits can be difficult for newborns. It can be hard to get a baby's head through the neck hole, and the shirts can rise up easily. Consider sticking to one-piece outfits in the beginning.*

Bottles and Nipples – There are so many different types of bottles, the choices can be overwhelming. How do you know which ones you should get? To be honest, because every baby is different, you might have to deal with a bit of trial and error here. Some babies may take to a bottle instantly, with no problems whatsoever. Other babies might be fussy and refuse to feed from certain nipples or bottles. Here are a few basic tips for choosing the right feeding tools:

- **Nipple sizes** – Nipples have different-sized holes to control the amount of liquid that flows from them. They're marked with the suggested age range, but again, every child is different—so don't be concerned if your baby doesn't follow the exact recommendation. You'll want to start with a small nipple size in the beginning, for a slower flow. The nipple might be too big if you notice a lot of milk or formula spilling out the sides of your baby's mouth during feedings, or if he or she is choking and spitting up. If your baby looks like they are sucking fiercely and getting frustrated during the feeding, you may need to jump up to the next nipple size to allow for a faster flow.

- **Nipple Shapes and Textures** – There are generally two types of nipples: latex or silicone. Latex nipples are softer and more flexible, while silicone ones are more firm. The shape can vary too, from round bulbs to ones that are flat on one side. The flat ones are said to feel more like a woman's breast and are supposedly better orthodontically. Babies can be extremely picky about the shape and texture of bottle nipples, so it's a good idea to hold off on stocking up until you've found one that works well. Try one type out for a few days and if it doesn't work, switch it out.

- **Bottle Shapes** – Some bottles are straight; other bottles are angled, supposedly to make them ergonomic and easier to hold. And while no one really knows what causes colic (excessive and inconsolable crying for no apparent reason in a baby who is otherwise considered healthy), some bottles with angled tops and special venting features can reduce gas and spit-up by limiting the amount of air that flows through. Widths on bottles vary too. Wider openings are easier for pouring formula and are easier to clean.

- **Bottle Materials** – Bottles are most commonly made out of plastic or glass.

  - Plastic is inexpensive, light, and shatterproof. There used to be a concern about plastic bottles having a chemical in them called Bisphenol A (BPA), but the Food and Drug Administration (FDA) banned its use in baby bottles and cups back in 2012.

  - Glass bottles are heavier and more expensive than the plastic ones, but they last longer. You can even get special sleeves to go over them to protect the bottle from shattering, if that's a concern you have.

  - Silicone and stainless steel bottles are also available, but these are slightly more expensive and harder to find. Since plastic and glass are easier to find when you need last-minute replacements, it might make more sense to go with one of those. To make things easier for you, make sure the bottles and nipples you buy are dishwasher safe.

TIP:
You're going to need about 8-12 bottles. The smaller four-ounce bottles are perfect for the amount a newborn will drink in one sitting–but babies grow quickly, and it won't be long before they will need to eat more. Skipping the smaller bottles and going straight for the bigger ones could save you money.

Formula – There are various types of formulas aimed to reduce spit-up, fussiness, gas, and colic. There are also specialized formulas for premature or low-birth-weight babies, and even ones for babies allergic to soy or milk. See page 107 for a complete rundown on formulas, and to get a better understanding for which type you should get. Remember, babies can be picky, and you may have to experiment until you find a formula that works well for them, so don't stock up until you've pinned down one your baby likes. Also, don't change formula types frequently. If your baby is being fussy with what they eat, consult your pediatrician and ask for their recommendation.

Bottle Brush – You're going to be spending a lot of time cleaning bottles, and since they come in various shapes, cleaning them can be difficult without a bottle brush. Get one. You'll thank me for it later.

Burp Cloths – You're going to get puked on a lot and will probably go through about ten to twelve burp cloths a day. They're great because they're thick, absorbent, and small enough to fit a few of them in a diaper bag.

Receiving Blankets and Swaddling Blankets – Receiving blankets are like swaddling blankets, except they are a bit smaller. Most, but not all, newborns like to be swaddled (wrapped snugly in cloth), because it keeps them confined like they were in the womb. It's familiar and comforting for them. These blankets are good for more than swaddling though. They can be draped over strollers to keep the sun out of your baby's eyes, or even used to cover public changing tables. It's good to start with three to six of these. You can always buy more if you need them.

Place to Sleep – Your baby is going to need a place to sleep, and the American Academy of Pediatrics recommends they sleep in the same bedroom as their parents (but not on the same surface) for the first six to twelve months, in order to reduce the risk of Sudden Infant Death Syndrome (SIDS). Babies should sleep on their backs, on a firm surface such as a cradle, crib, or bassinet. Cradles and bassinets might make things easier for you in the beginning since they are more portable and easier to move from room to room. Also, consider a Pack 'n Play for the first few months prior to transitioning to a crib. Some even come with a convenient side-by-side bassinet and changing table, which can be a huge help for middle-of-the-night diaper changes.

Fitted Sheets – It's important that sheets fit tightly in whatever sleeping space you use, because loose bedding can increase the risk of SIDS. Since babies can spit-up a lot, consider getting four or five fitted sheets.

Blankets – It's possible that you can get away with just using swaddling blankets if you're in a warmer climate, but you may want to get a couple of blankets for the car seat or stroller just in case. Only use them if your baby is buckled in and can't move around. Blankets should always be snug and secure. Never use a loose blanket for your baby while he or she is sleeping, because it can increase the risk of SIDS.

Sleep Sacks – Since you shouldn't use blankets while your baby is sleeping, consider getting a few sleep sacks. They cover your baby's body and keep them warm while they're sleeping. Make sure you get the right size. It's important that you don't get ones that are too tight or too loose.

Bibs – These will work in conjunction with burp cloths to catch spit-up and drool. Consider getting four or five of these in the beginning since they'll get dirty quickly. Keep in mind that, just like clothes, you will need to get bigger sizes as your baby grows.

Diaper Bag – If you ever want to leave the house, you're going to want to get a diaper bag. This is going to hold everything you could possibly need while on the road: diapers, changes of clothes, bottles, toys, you name it. Basically, it's your magical British nanny bag. They come in different sizes and styles, and since times are changing, they're not all in bright pink or floral print anymore. Designers have started to cater to fathers and have created diaper bags that come in camouflage, branded with your favorite sports teams, and more. Some are made as backpacks and even murses/man bags. You can do a quick search for "diaper bags for dad" online and you'll see a ton of options. A word of advice though: this is another instance where substance beats style. Practicality is important. You want a bag that's easy to use so you can find things when you're in a hurry. Easy access to diapers, wipes, and bottles is more important than looking like a fashion model.

Stroller – This is another item you're going to need if you ever want to leave the house. Technically, you can hold your baby the whole time you're out, but if you ever want to get a break (and you will), a stroller is going to come in handy. Again, there are so many different types that choosing the best one can be overwhelming, and while jogging daddies can be sexy, are you really going to be using that jogging stroller, or are you going to give that up like a New Year's resolution in February? The thing with strollers is that none of them are perfect for every situation, so the key to getting a good stroller is finding one that fits your lifestyle. Here are a few questions you should ask yourself before splurging on one:

1. What is your budget? Strollers can range from about $25 to over $1,000! Keep in mind that more expensive does not always mean better. The most important thing is whether or not it fits your lifestyle.

2. Will you be traveling a lot? If you're going to be taking the stroller on trips, think about how easily it folds up and how much space it's going to take in the car. Will it fit with all your other luggage?

3. Will you have to carry it a lot? If you're going to be going up and down a lot of stairs, or constantly lifting it in and out of a car, you're probably not going to want the heaviest stroller.

4. Are you and your partner the same height? If not, you may want to get a stroller with adjustable handlebars.

5. Do you want a car seat that clips into your stroller? Some strollers come with a car seat that clips in and

out, making it easy to transfer from the stroller to the car or vice versa with ease. This will also make it less likely that you'll wake your sleeping baby while getting in and out of the car.

6. What kind of terrain will you be on? Your terrain will determine which type of wheel is best for you. Plastic wheels are fine for smooth surfaces like sidewalks and tile, but they may struggle elsewhere. Air-filled tires are great everywhere as long as you don't get a flat. They're like bicycle tires. Foam-filled tires are great in any situation. Also, consider the suspension: the more suspension, the better your stroller will handle various terrains and the less likely your baby will wake up while traveling on bumpy roads.

7. How easy will it be to keep clean? If you're going to be using the stroller a lot, you're going to want something that is easy to clean. Check to see if the seat is removable and washable. Can it be wiped down easily?

8. Do you need a lot of storage? Not all strollers are equal when it comes to storage space. Make sure there's enough for what you need.

9. What types of accessories does it have? Do you need cup holders? Snack trays? Rain covers? Don't fret if you found the perfect stroller without these. You can probably buy an accessory separately.

Baby Carrier -- Strollers are not always the most practical mode of transportation for your baby. For example, if you're pushing a stroller around the grocery store, how are you going to be able to push a shopping cart around too? Baby carriers are amazing for situations like these! They cuddle your little one against your body, keeping your arms free to do various other things like grocery shopping or folding laundry. Just be sure to avoid chores that require movements that could put your child in harm's way.

There are many different types of baby carriers out there. For men, the most popular type of carrier is a buckle carrier, because they are comfortable, convenient, and easy to use. Most are versatile and can be worn in front or on your back like a backpack. When picking a carrier, make sure you get one that is adjustable and can grow with your child. Also, make sure your carrier is appropriate for your child's weight. Some carriers come with special infant inserts for smaller babies to make sure they are properly secured.

First-Aid Kit – You can buy pre-packaged first-aid kits that pretty much come with everything you need. At a minimum, make sure you have the following:

- A digital thermometer (and petroleum jelly if it's a rectal thermometer)
- Baby non-aspirin liquid pain reliever. Ask a pediatrician or pharmacist what they recommend.
- Saline drops to loosen mucus
- A bulb syringe to clear mucus from a stuffy nose
- Antibacterial ointment for minor cuts and scrapes
- Tweezers
- Adhesive bandages in various sizes

Because you can never be too prepared, here are a few other items you may want to include in your baby's first aid kit:

- Sunscreen
- Mild liquid soap
- Rubbing alcohol for cleaning thermometers

- Scissors

- Cotton balls

- A heating pad

- Instant cold pack

- Emergency foil blanket

- Eye wash

- Electrolyte solution for hydration after vomiting or diarrhea. Use only if your pediatrician advises you to do so.

- Microporous adhesive tape

- Gauze pads and gauze rolls

- Hydrocortisone cream

- Vinyl gloves

- First-aid manual

Always follow the directions on the packaging and use the recommended dosages for any medicines.

Toiletries – We all know the importance of staying well groomed, and your baby is no exception. The good thing is that you'll only need a few key items.

- **Baby Wash** – You'll need a gentle liquid or foam bath wash for your baby. Their skin is sensitive, so you'll want to avoid anything heavily fragranced. Some come in hypoallergenic and fragrance-free formulas. Some even come in a convenient two-in-one shampoo and body wash combo.

- **Shampoo** – Make sure the shampoo is tear-free in case it accidentally gets in your infant's eyes.

- **Baby Tub** – This isn't a necessity, but a good tub helps a lot! Babies can be slippery when wet, especially if you have used oil or cream on their skin. A baby tub helps to keep a baby in place while you bathe them. Some tubs are made to fit in the sink so you're not straining your back while bending over a full-sized tub. Other baby tubs are designed to fit inside a regular tub, and some are even designed to accommodate your baby while he or she grows. Look for tubs that provide support for your baby's head and have a nonskid bottom, both on the inside, for your baby, and on the outside, to prevent the tub from moving around.

- **Nail Clippers** – You'll find yourself trimming your little wolverine's nails often. They grow fast and they're sharp as razors too! Cutting your little one's nails for the first time can be intimidating because babies squirm a lot, but don't worry. You'll get used to it. You'll need a set of baby clippers, because adult clippers are too dangerous to use on infants. Some come with built-in magnifiers and/or lights to help make it easier to see what you're doing.

- **Moisturizers and Oils** – Baby skin can get dry easily, but a gentle lotion can help keep them moisturized. Coconut oil works great too. No need to soak them in it, but it's good to use every once in a while.

TIP:
Baby oil or coconut oil can help clean off sticky poop.

- **Diaper Rash Cream** – You'll need this to help ease your little one's pain when their bottom gets sore. A little goes a long way though, so use just a dab at a time.

- **Pacifiers** – These come in various different shapes and sizes, and you might have to try a few different ones until your baby finds a pacifier they like. Some pacifier nipples are bulb shaped; others are rounded with flat bottoms. The bases come in different shapes too. When you find one your baby likes, stock up on a few so you have spares. Also, it's handy to find ones that are dishwasher safe.

Things That Are Good to Have But Are Not Mandatory

Changing Pads – You can change your baby on the bed or couch, but small changing pads have the benefit of being soft, portable, and convenient. Technically, you can also just put a towel on the floor to keep the mess contained, but towels don't provide as much cushion.

Baby Swing – These are wonderful, because they free up your hands to do chores around the house like cleaning, dishes, laundry, cooking, etc. Not all babies will like the rocking motion of the swing, but many are comforted by it. If you get a swing, make sure your baby meets the weight requirements and can be strapped in securely.

Baby Monitor – If your house is on the smaller side, you may be able to hear your child cry no matter what room you're in, but if your house is bigger and has multiple floors, hearing your child in the middle of the night may prove to be a bit more difficult. Baby monitors alert you if your infant becomes active while you are in another room. Some are audio only, some have sound with a light indicator, and others come with cameras so you can hear and see your baby. There are even options to use your phone as a baby monitor, but keep practicality in mind and think about what happens if you have to take a call.

Things You Don't Need to Buy

Bottle Sterilizers – Previously, people needed to sterilize bottles before every use. Now, pediatricians say that if the water is safe enough to drink, then it's safe enough for cleaning. Some doctors recommend sterilizing bottles and nipples before the first use, but there is no evidence saying you have to. If you use well water, get it checked for impurities and make sure it is safe to drink. If there are any concerns with the quality of your water, then you may want to get a bottle sterilizer. Otherwise, you can just sterilize bottles when you need to by putting them in boiling water for five minutes.

Wipe Warmers – Some parents swear by these, but honestly, you don't need them. Keep in mind, if you start warming wipes, your baby will get used to it and expect all wipes to be warm from that point on. Do you really want to carry a travel warmer with you everywhere you go? It's just another thing to pack in the diaper bag and it takes a while to warm up too. Trust me. Skip the wipe warmer. If you think a wipe is too cold, you can always hold it between the palms of your hands for a few seconds to warm it up.

Bottle Warmers – While a warm bottle may be nice, a baby doesn't need heated formula. Room temperature is fine. Once you start warming the bottles, your baby will expect all bottles to be warm and may get fussy if given formula at a different temperature. Think about how this will impact feeding on the go. You may want to get a portable travel warmer if you go somewhere outside where the temperature will make the formula cold. Other than that, you can skip these and save the money.

Baby Towels – While baby towels can be cute, and the hooded ones can keep your baby's head warm, they're not a necessity. You can use a regular towel to dry your baby off after a bath. Just make sure the towel is soft. The same goes for washcloths.

Diaper Pails – These may sound great, and some parents swear by them, but you don't need one. Diaper pails are like mini trash cans for diapers with lids that hold in the dirty stench. The problem with these is that they take special liners that can get expensive quickly, and while it's true that the smell gets trapped in the can, just think about what the smell is like when it's time to empty the bag full of stinky diapers. Consider wrapping a soiled diaper in a doggy poop bag if you can't put it in an outside trashcan right away. Doggie poop bags are also great for changing dirty diapers on the go when you're away from the house and there isn't a trashcan nearby. Just bag the dirty diaper until you're at a place where you can properly dispose of it.

Pee Blockers – Seriously? While the concept may sound cute and useful, they're pointless. These whizz blockers are supposed to prevent baby boys from spraying you during diaper changes, but, in reality, they're hard to stay put on a squirming baby, and you'll most likely wind up getting peed on anyway. Putting a washcloth or second diaper over the crotch area can help if you're that worried about it. You don't need a special device.

Pacifier Wipes – You don't need special wipes to clean pacifiers that have fallen on the ground. Just run them under water to clean them or keep a few spares handy.

Baby Landry Soap – This is an example of clever marketing. You absolutely do not need special "baby laundry soap." Just use natural laundry soap, or something fragrance free or hypoallergenic. You can use this soap for all the clothes in the household.

Newborn Mittens – Again, these look cute and it may sound like you need them to keep your baby from scratching themselves. Unfortunately, they don't stay on well. If keeping your baby's nails trimmed isn't solving the issue, there are long-sleeved baby outfits available with tiny hand pockets at the end of the sleeves. Another option is to try putting baby socks over their hands, but again, those may not stay on.

Shoes – While they may look cute, babies don't need shoes until they start walking. Plus, they're restraining and may not even stay on. Save the money and wait to get shoes for when your baby is older.

Shopping Cart Covers – Shopping carts are so dirty and covered in germs! Who wouldn't want to protect their baby from them? Well guess what, the world is full of germs everywhere you go and unless you plan on raising your baby in a plastic bubble, he or she is going to come in contact with them. You don't need a special shopping cart cover to protect your baby while they sit in the grocery cart. Plus, who wants to drag one of those with them every time they go shopping anyway? If you are really that worried about it, use a wipe to wipe the cart down before seating your kid in one.

Baby Kneepads – Babies are so fragile. Wouldn't kneepads be great for protecting their little knees while they're learning how to crawl? Umm, no. They're babies, not professional skateboarders. Unless you're raising a mini Tony Hawk, you don't need baby kneepads.

Bathtub Thermometer – If you have no concept of what lukewarm means and you have an irrational fear that you're going to boil your baby alive, by all means get a bathtub thermometer. Otherwise, use your wrist or elbow to make sure the water is lukewarm.

Crib Bedding Sets – Bedding sets are cute, but you know what? They're also expensive. Plus, your baby's crib really shouldn't have most of the things that come in those sets anyway. The American Academy of Pediatrics says that blankets, comforters, pillows, crib bumpers, and soft toys increase the risk of SIDS, so you're better having your infant sleep prison-style, with a mattress and fitted sheet only.

Baby Powder – Baby powder used to be a staple in many houses across the country. It was used to prevent diaper rash, but has since become controversial in regards to safety. Diaper rash creams are safer for treating diaper rash, and you don't have to worry about your baby inhaling the powder from the air either.

When the Baby is Born – Creating a Birth Plan

If you are expanding your family via open adoption or surrogacy, chances are you're going to need a birth plan. A birth plan is a document that you'll collaboratively work on with the birthmother or surrogate to make sure everything goes smoothly during your time in the hospital.

This may be an extremely difficult time for birthmothers because the hospital makes the whole adoption more real. Even if you agreed to have a lot of contact going forward, she may feel like she is losing her baby. Because of this, compassion and understanding are crucial when you're making this plan. You may already have certain expectations in your head for how you want things to go, but when you're creating the birth plan with a birthmother, try to consider her point of view as well, so she doesn't feel obligated to do things she's uncomfortable with. Emotions will be all over the place, so it helps to have a well-thought-out plan to make things less stressful for everyone. Here are a few things to consider when creating your birth plan.

- Does the birthmother or surrogate have a preference for which hospital they would like to go to? If so, try to contact them ahead of time to let them know about your situation. It's important for the hospital to know that the birth is going to be an adoption or surrogacy so they will have an understanding of who will be present. Make sure you share your birth plan with the hospital as well, so things can run as smoothly as possible.

- Where will you be staying during the birth? Surrogates and birthmothers may not live near you. Check out the hotels ahead of time if you have the chance. For an open adoption, you may be staying in a hotel for a few weeks, so it's a good idea to make sure you have a variety of food options near by.

- What will you be taking to the hospital with you? At a minimum, you're going to need a car seat, because most hospitals will not discharge a baby without one. You might want to bring one or two outfits (for the baby, not you), a swaddling blanket, and a couple of diapers with you, too. Feel free to bring a couple of bottles of formula as well, if you think you'll need it.

- Does the birthmother or surrogate prefer a natural birth or a C-section? You're not the one physically giving birth, so you are probably not going to have much input on this, but it's important to understand how the birthmother or surrogate plans to have the baby. Keep in mind, even if she plans on giving birth a certain way, there may be circumstances where the plan has to change.

- Will there be a midwife or doula present?

- Does the birthmother or surrogate want medication during the birth?

- Who will be in the room during the birth? Maybe you want to be in the room to witness this once-in-a-lifetime moment. Maybe you're not sure if you can handle it and would rather stay in the waiting room. If you'd prefer to witness the birth, keep in mind that in regards to open adoption, this is a vulnerable moment for the birthmother. She may feel awkward, exposed, and uncomfortable with you present in the delivery room while she's dressed in a hospital gown with her legs up in the air. Make sure she doesn't feel pressured to do something she doesn't want to do. Also, if the birth is going to be a C-section, the hospital might have restrictions on how many people can be in the room.

- Who will cut the umbilical cord? Will there be cord blood banking and/or delayed cord clamping?

- Who will be the first to hold the baby?

- Will there be pictures or video allowed in the hospital? If so, when and where? Will the birthmother or surrogate be in any pictures with the baby?

- Who will primarily be with the baby during the hospital stay?

- Will the baby's first feeding be breast milk or formula? If it is decided that the baby will have breast milk, will the birthmother or surrogate breastfeed, or will she pump?

- If you are doing an open adoption, will the birthmother have alone time with the baby?

- Establish who will be making decisions regarding the baby's health while in the hospital.

- Who will give the baby their first bath? Your baby will get a bath while in the hospital. The nurses may be the ones to do this, or they may allow one of you to do it.

- If the baby is a boy, will he be circumcised?

- Who will be allowed to visit the baby in the hospital? Will it just be you and the birthmother/surrogate, or do you want friends and family members there too? Does the birthmother/surrogate want friends or family members present for support? Is there anyone that should not be allowed to visit?

- Who will choose the baby's name on the birth certificate?

- Whose names will appear as the parents on the birth certificate? Laws regarding this vary from state to state.

- Make it very clear where you want the original birth certificate sent. In the case of adoption, the birthmother may not want to receive a birth certificate in the mail.

- Who will take home hospital mementos, like baby ID bracelets?

- What happens when it's time to leave the hospital? For birthmothers, some may want to leave before the baby is discharged, while others may want to leave with the adoptive family. Who will carry the baby out?

Keep in mind that the birth plan is designed to help things run more smoothly during the hectic time at the hospital. It is a living document, and things can change. It's possible that an emergency C-section may be required, thus altering who can be in the room. Or maybe you bond more with the birthmother over time, and things change because you are more comfortable with each other. Be as detailed and honest as you can when creating this document, but be open for changes down the road.

Circumcision

If your baby is born with a penis, one of the first major decisions you will have to make is whether or not you are going to circumcise your child. While it used to be automatically assumed that newborn males in the United States would be circumcised, the percentage of infants getting circumcised has significantly dropped over the last few years. Some insurance companies have even stopped covering the procedure because it is not a necessity. Ultimately, it's your choice whether or not you want to circumcise your baby, but if you're having trouble making the decision, here are some of the reasons people choose to go through the procedure or not:

Reasons Why People Choose to Circumcise	Reasons Why People Choose Not to Circumcise
Religion – Some parents choose to circumcise their babies because their faith tells them to.	**Lack of Medical Necessity** – The health benefits for circumcision are so minute, many wonder if they are enough to justify surgically removing part of an infant's body.
Tradition – Some parents choose to circumcise their babies because the fathers are circumcised.	**Tradition** – Some parents choose to not circumcise their babies because the fathers are not circumcised.
Cleanliness – Some people believe a circumcised penis is easier to clean, although that's not entirely accurate. For the first few years of life, the foreskin is stuck to the head of the penis by connective tissue that will dissolve naturally, so all you have to do is wipe the outside of the penis with a wipe during diaper changes, or a washcloth/sponge when your baby is in the bath. Never attempt to retract a child's foreskin for cleaning. When the inside surface separates from the head of the penis and the foreskin's opening widens, it can be pulled back for easy cleaning.	**Consent** – Some people believe it is unfair to force a surgery on a child when it is not medically necessary. They say it is best to wait until the child is old enough to make the decision on their own, but it's important to note there is a higher risk of complications when performing circumcision on older children and adults.

Teasing – Some parents fear their sons will get teased in the locker room if their penis looks different from everyone else's. Keep in mind though: circumcision rates in the United States have dropped, so this may not be that big of an issue as time goes by.

Pain – Circumcision involves surgically removing skin from a sensitive part of the body, so there will definitely be pain. While there is pain relief that can be used, some people are uncomfortable putting that stress on a newborn baby.

Health – Uncircumcised males have a higher rate of urinary tract infections (UTIs) and penile cancer, but the percentages are so small: about 1 percent for UTIs and much smaller for penile cancer, which is already rare in the United States. Plus, we now have a vaccine that can prevent most, but not all, penile cancers.

Cost – Some insurance companies have stopped covering the cost of circumcision, and some parents choose to not incur additional costs.

Preventing HIV/AIDS – There have been studies that have shown circumcised males are less likely to contract HIV; however, the findings have been strongly contested. Most of the studies were conducted in Africa and only looked at adult subjects who had heterosexual sex. They didn't measure other risks and behaviors, such as condom usage, drug use, needle sharing, male-male sex, etc. Because there are so many different factors involved, it's important to note that correlation does not mean causation.

Feeding Your Baby –
No Boobie, No Problem

Newborn babies eat a lot, like every two to three hours, but with so many different options for what to feed them, how do you know what's best? Is formula OK, or should you opt for milk through a breast milk bank? And if you choose formula, what's the best kind? When should you switch to solids? Here you'll find the basics for feeding your baby so you can make an informed decision on how you want to proceed.

Donor Breast Milk vs. Formula

There are claims out there that breast milk is better for babies than formula because it's natural. Depending on whom you talk to, you may hear that breastfed babies are smarter and less likely to get diseases, but Dr. Raymond Cattaneo, a pediatrician in Kansas City, Missouri says we need to critically assess the claims.

For example, the Journal of the American Medical Association published a meta-analysis study in 2015 by Efrat L. Amitay, PhD, MPH and Lital Keinan-Boker, MD, PhD, MPH, which indicated that breastfeeding for six months or more "may" help lower the risk of childhood leukemia. The study showed the number of childhood leukemia cases decreased by 0.8 per 100,000, but guess what? There are so many other factors (the family's history of cancer, the breastfeeding woman's weight, whether or not she smoked, different environmental exposures, etc.) to take into consideration when comparing women who breastfeed to women who don't, that it's almost impossible to identify what is contributing to what. Also, much of the data was collected by having women complete a self-administered questionnaire, therefore introducing a potential recall bias. So, while the study showed that breastfeeding "may" reduce the risk of childhood leukemia, it didn't prove that it absolutely does, nor did it prove that breastfeeding is best.

So if you're looking for medical research to determine if you should feed your child breast milk or formula, there's honestly not enough information out there to determine whether one is conclusively better than the other. Formula has come a long way over the past few years, and as long as your baby is getting the proper nutrients, they should be fine. "When I see a child at five, six, ten, or fifteen years of age, I can't tell who was breastfed, who was formula fed, or who was fed both," says Dr. Cattaneo. "I don't tell people one is better than the other. My motto is 'Fed is best.'"

If you choose to move forward with formula, there are instances where some babies will have issues with certain types. They may get irritable, gassy, or fussy, or they may spit up a lot. This doesn't necessarily mean you should switch to breast milk. There are various types of formula, so you may have to experiment until you find a formula that works well for your baby. Keep in mind, there's a difference between the taste and consistency of formula and that of breast milk. If you switch between the two, your baby might become fussy, refuse to feed, arch their back, or more—so switching back and forth is not recommended. If your baby is being fussy with what they eat, consult your pediatrician and ask for their recommendation.

One final thing to seriously take into consideration is that donor milk from breast milk banks is expensive. You're looking at four to eight dollars per ounce, plus shipping! That price tag alone is enough to make the donor option out of reach for some families. Ultimately, choosing between breast milk and formula is a personal choice for parents, and there is no right or wrong answer. Just make sure your baby is getting the proper nutrients. Again, if there are any concerns with your baby's feeding, you should consult with their pediatrician.

Breast Milk Banks

If you decide to feed your infant donor milk, you can look online for a breast milk bank near you. A good resource is the Human Milk Banking Association of North America (HMBANA). They are a professional association that issues voluntary safety guidelines on screening breast milk donors, in addition to collecting, processing, handling, testing, and storing milk. More information about HMBANA can be found on their website at www.hmbana.org. Don't worry if you're not within driving distance of a breast milk bank, since most places will ship the milk directly to you.

There are possible health and safety risks for your baby if you feed them human milk from a source other than their birthmother. You could potentially expose your child to infectious diseases and/or chemical contaminants, like illegal or prescription drugs. Also, if breast milk is not handled and stored properly, it could become contaminated and unsafe for your child to drink. A few states have put in place required safety standards for breast milk banks, but the US Food and Drug Administration has not been involved in establishing those state standards. Dr. Cattaneo says that if you choose to go with donor milk, you should only use milk from a source that has screened its milk donors and has taken other precautions to ensure the milk is safe. Don't select random donors from online networks or get breast milk from a friend of a friend.

Formula

Choosing a formula for the first time can be overwhelming. There are lots of options, so to help you in your decision, here's a rundown of the different types available:

Powdered Formula – Powdered formula is the cheapest option, so if you're looking to keep costs down, this is the way to go. It does require a lot of measuring and mixing, though.

Concentrated Liquid Formula – This is a liquid that you dilute with water. It's a little more expensive than powder, and you'll still be measuring and mixing.

Ready-to-Use Liquid Formula – This is the most convenient option, because the water is already mixed in and the liquid can be poured right into the bottle. This can be handy when you're traveling and can't find a sterile water supply, but this type of formula is also the most expensive option.

After choosing what type works best for you, now it's time to choose what kind works for your baby. Most infants can do well on a regular, cow's-milk-based formula, so that is a good place to start unless your pediatrician says otherwise. It has a good balance of carbohydrates, fat, and protein. If your baby is spitting up a lot, try changing the way you feed. For example, keep them upright longer after a feeding, try switching bottle types, or burp them more. If they still seem to have trouble eating after about a week or two, consult your pediatrician and ask for recommendations. Here are a few other kinds of formulas:

TIP:
Even though some formula is cow's milk based, it is
significantly altered so that babies can digest it. Infants
cannot properly digest cow's milk for a while, and it is
not recommended to give a baby cow's milk until after
their first birthday.

Partially Hydrolyzed Formulas – With these, the protein is broken down to make them easier for babies to digest. This type of formula helps babies that have trouble absorbing nutrients.

Soy-Based Formula – This formula may be a good option for infants allergic to cow's milk; however, if they are allergic to the protein in cow's milk, they may also be allergic to the protein in soy-based formula. Consult a pediatrician before using this kind of formula. Also consult a pediatrician if you notice wheezing, hives, or rashes after feeding.

Premature Baby Formula – This formula typically contains more calories and protein, as well as a fat that's easily absorbed. If your baby is born premature or has a low birth weight, ask your pediatrician which formula is best to use.

Organic Formula – There is no research to date that proves organic formula is better than non-organic formula, so you will need to think about whether or not it makes sense to pay the higher price.

How Much Should I Feed My Baby?

For the first week, ease your baby into feeding by giving them one to two ounces every three to four hours, but never give them more than what they want. Take your baby's cue. After the first week, you can ease them up to about two to three ounces every three to four hours. As your baby gets bigger, they'll slowly increase the amount of formula or breast milk they eat. Every baby is different, but a good rule of thumb is to feed them approximately two and a half ounces of formula per pound of body weight each day. So if your baby is eight pounds, they'll eat about twenty ounces in a twenty-four-hour period. The frequency for how often they eat will slowly decrease as the quantity gets larger. Below is a good guide for the average baby, but check with your pediatrician to make sure you have a good feeding schedule for your child and that they are getting the right amount of nutrients.

Age	Bottles Per Day	Amount in Each Bottle	Total Amount Per Day
Newborn	6–8	2–3 oz.	12–24 oz.
1-2 Months	6–8	4 oz.	24–32 oz.
3-4 Months	6	4–6 oz.	24–36 oz.
5-6 Months	5	6–8 oz.	30–40 oz.
7-9 Months	3–4, in addition to solids	7–8 oz.	21–32 oz.
10-12 Months	2–3, in addition to solids	8 oz.	16–24 oz.

When Can My Baby Have Juice?

The American Academy of Pediatrics recommends that juice should not be introduced into a child's diet until after they are a year old, and even then, should be limited to four ounces a day. Dr. Cattaneo says parents should avoid juice altogether, if possible, because it provides no health benefits whatsoever, even if it says otherwise on the bottle. Most fruit juices have a high sugar content, lack dietary fiber, and may even contribute to excessive weight gain. Rather than drinking juice, children should be encouraged to eat whole fruits and vegetables. If you do wind up giving your child juice, make sure they drink it out of a sippy cup rather than a bottle to lessen the risk of tooth decay. Also, make sure it is 100 percent fruit juice with no added sugar. It's important to realize "no added sugar" can still have a hell of a lot of sugar.

TIP:
You can lower the sugar content in juice by watering it down: half juice and half water. This will also give you peace of mind, knowing that your kid is less likely to run around like a raging lunatic from a sugar high, and that even if they do, it probably won't last as long as it would have if you hadn't watered it down.

When Can My Baby Have Water?

Free water (that is, water not mixed in formula or already in breast milk) can cause electrolyte imbalances in babies, leading to seizures, coma, and even death. That is also why it is vitally important not to dilute formula which is designed to be mixed in a certain way. Using less formula and more water to save money can cause the same electrolyte imbalances.

It is ok to introduce free water in a sippy cup to infants six to nine months old. Limit it to about four ounces a day, and only allow them to have a few sips at a time to prevent them from getting too full or from getting a tummy ache. It is important they still get the necessary nutrients found in milk or formula. After they are a year old and well into eating solid foods, they can have more water. Check with your pediatrician if you have questions or concerns.

When Should We Introduce Solid Foods?

The American Academy of Pediatrics recommends that you introduce solids sometime between four and six months of age. Check with your pediatrician before introducing solid foods to make sure your baby is ready. Signs that your baby may be ready to try solid foods include:

- The ability to hold their head up on their own. They have good head control and can eat in a sitting position.

- Their extrusion reflex, where they push food on their tongue to the front of their mouth, has mostly disappeared.

- They become curious about other foods. Maybe they watch you eat or try to grab your food.

When we first introduce solid foods into an infant's diet, it's more about training them how to eat than about making sure they get more nutrients. It's also about teaching them different food textures, what to do with their tongues, and how to push food into the back of their mouths. The majority of nutrients should still come from breast milk or formula, and solid foods should compliment a bottled feeding in the beginning, not replace it. Also, when introducing new foods, only do one at a time. This makes it easier for your baby to digest and will also help you identify any foods your child may be allergic to.

Rice cereal made specifically for babies is a good place to start when introducing solids. For the first few times, try giving your baby a little formula, followed by half teaspoons of rice cereal (mixed with formula). After a couple of teaspoons, end the meal with a little bit of formula again.

Dr. Cattaneo says you don't have to limit yourself to rice cereal as a first food though. Pediatricians used to recommend it because they thought that cereal was the least likely to cause allergies. They later found out this is not necessarily true. He says a first food could pretty much be anything in pureed form, as long as it's not listed in the "What Foods Should Be Avoided" section below. Some people find that mild fruits and vegetables like pureed apples, bananas, carrots, and peas are good first foods, but you can even try some meats like pureed beef, chicken, turkey, and lamb.

Around eight to ten months, you can start giving combinations of foods, but you still only want to introduce one new food at a time. Your baby may be able to handle heartier foods, such as pureed broccoli, asparagus, and apricots. When your baby is able to sit up on their own, reach for food, and put it in their mouth, they may be ready to try other solid foods like wafer-type cookies and crackers. Around ten to twelve months, your baby may be ready for pasta and small chunks or pieces of food that can easily be mashed in their mouth.

What Foods Should Be Avoided?

There are many different types of foods that you should hold off on feeding your child, many which are listed below. When introducing your child to new foods, think about how they may eat it. Is the food easy enough to chew without teeth? Is it small enough to swallow without getting lodged in their throats? For the first few years, food should be cut into pieces no larger than half an inch. Below is a list of food items to avoid until your child is about three or four years old unless otherwise specified.

Cow's Milk – Cow's milk should not be introduced into your child's diet until they are one year old because before then, they won't be able to properly digest the protein in it. When you do introduce milk, avoid low fat because most children need the fat and calories for proper growth and development. Only feed your child low-fat milk if your pediatrician recommends it, which they may if your child is at risk for obesity.

Honey and Corn Syrup – Wait until your child is at least one year old before giving them honey or corn syrup, because it may contain spores of bacteria that can cause botulism.

Nuts and Seeds – These can be choking hazards, so hold off on feeding your little one nuts and seeds, such as peanuts, almonds, sunflower seeds, pumpkin seeds, etc. Also, make sure you carefully remove seeds and pits from fresh fruits.

Raw Vegetables – Cook vegetables to make them softer and easier to eat.

Whole Grapes – Grapes can be choking hazards when eaten whole. Cut them into halves or quarters.

Hard and Crunchy Foods – Avoid foods like popcorn, pretzels, mints, and hard candies, which can get lodged in your child's throat.

Peanut Butter – Nut butters of any kind can be difficult to swallow and can be a choking hazard. Avoid giving them to your child in large dollops or on a spoon. If you want your child to have peanut butter or another kind of nut butter, spread it thinly on something like bread or crackers.

Cheese – Avoid cheese that's stringy or melted, because it can be a choking hazard.

The above list is just a guide, and you should always check with your pediatrician before introducing new foods. Remember to wait several days after each new food item before introducing a new one, so you can identify whether your child has any allergic reactions to any of them. Also, because of allergies, check with your pediatrician to see when they recommend introducing foods like eggs, fish, shellfish, soy, and nuts. Alert your pediatrician if you notice any reactions such as diarrhea, rashes, or vomiting to certain foods.

Should We Feed Our Baby Organic Food?

Dr. Cattaneo says there is no definitive research proving that eating organic foods (and/or non-GMO foods) is necessary to prevent infections, helps growth and development, or has any other proposed benefits. And similar to what he said about breast milk vs. formula, when he sees a child at five, six, ten, or fifteen years of age, he can't tell who ate organic foods and who didn't.

From a health standpoint, there's no risk to going organic, but you're probably not going to prevent infections any more or less. The same goes for GMO foods. The science shows they are safe. If you are buying a non-GMO product, you are paying for the label, not a health benefit. If you can afford buying organic food though, and you want to do it, go for it. Organic farming is probably better for the environment, so that may be something you may want to take into consideration. In the end, it's ultimately a personal decision for you to make.

There's More Than One Way to Burp a Baby

When your baby is feeding from a bottle, you should burp them about every two ounces or whenever they start getting fussy. We often see people holding babies over their shoulder while patting them on the back, but the truth is, there are different positions for burping your baby, and sometimes you may have to try more than one. Here are a few different burping positions:

On Your Shoulder – Rest your baby's head on your shoulder and keep them in position with one hand under their bottom and the other on their back. Use the hand on their back to gently rub up and down, hopefully releasing any trapped air bubbles. If your baby doesn't burp after about a minute, try patting their back for a minute. Go back and forth between rubbing and patting until you are successful.

Sitting Up – Sit your baby on your lap. Use the thumb and pointer finger of one hand to hold the chin up and support their head. The base of your hand and wrist can be used to support your baby's chest and shoulders. Place your other hand on your baby's back and slowly lean them forward a bit so they are at a slight angle. Alternate between rubbing and patting your baby's back, while making sure their head does not flop around.

Lying Down – Place your baby across your lap facedown so their head is over one of your legs and their tummy is over the other. Hold them securely with one hand and use the other hand to rub or pat their back.

What If My Baby Is Constipated?

Every baby will poop on a different schedule, and that is usually OK. They may poop seven times in a day, or go several days without a bowel movement. They may even strain and turn purple while pooping, and that could be OK too. For a healthy child, constipation is defined by the consistency of the stool: hard, round pellets. Other signs may include straining for more than ten minutes, increased spit-up, or decreased feeding.

Constipation in infants is common, especially when they start eating new solid foods. Prune juice is a natural laxative that helps soften the stool and can make it easier for your child to go when they are having trouble. Pedialyte is another good option. Both of them may work quicker for some babies than for others, depending on the severity of your child's constipation—or they may not work at all. Consult your pediatrician if your child has gone several days without producing a bowel movement, or is crying in pain while going to the bathroom.

TIP:

For children six months to a year old, try diluting one to two tablespoons of prune juice in two to three ounces of water or formula at first. Keep in mind, a little bit of prune juice goes a long way! You can always add more, but you can't add less. Giving your child too much prune juice can give them diarrhea for days and result in a very sore bottom.

Diapers

This section tells you everything you need to know about diapers: how to pick the right type, how to pick the right size, and how to properly change them. Did you know there are differences between changing a boy's diaper and changing a girl's? That's all covered here in addition to tips on what you can do when you can't find a changing table.

The Big Debate: Cloth vs. Disposable

If you have an infant, you're going to be dealing with a lot of diapers, so it's important to use a type that best fits your lifestyle. Both cloth and disposable diapers have their own pros and cons.

Cloth diapers are better for the environment and are cheaper than disposables, as long as you're doing your own laundry and not using a service that rents out cloth diapers, washes them, and delivers clean ones back to your house. The downside is that they are messier and not very convenient. When you change cloth diapers away from home, you will have to carry them back to your house so you can wash them later. So if your baby poops while you're at the beach, park, or mall, you'll be carrying that smelly diaper around with you until you're ready to go home.

Disposable diapers are less messy, more convenient, and easier to use, but they're also more expensive and worse for the environment. The fastening tabs on disposable diapers can also rip easily if you pull too hard, which sucks if you're away from home and only have one diaper left.

Still not sure which ones to go with? Ask other parents what they use and what their experience with diapers has been like. You can also do a quick search online to see what other people say.

	Cloth	Disposable
Pros	• They are cheaper than disposable diapers, as long as you're not using a cleaning service. • They are more natural, without all the dyes and gels used in disposable diapers. • They are better for the environment.	• They are easier to change and more convenient than cloth diapers. • They are more absorbent than cloth diapers, so you will be doing fewer changes. • They are not as messy as cloth diapers. • You will have less laundry to do, because you just throw away the dirty diapers instead of washing them.
Cons	• They are messier and harder to change. • You will have a lot more laundry to do. • You will be doing more diaper changes because they are less absorbent. • When you change diapers away from home, you'll have to carry them back home with you, even the really smelly ones.	• They are more expensive than cloth diapers. • They are bad for the environment because very little breaks down. • Fastening tabs can rip easily if you pull too hard.

Benefits	Cloth	Disposable
Can be cheaper	✓	
Better for the environment	✓	
Less messy		✓
Less laundry		✓
Easier to change		✓
More absorbent (fewer diaper changes)		✓
Fewer dyes and gels	✓	
May make potty training easier	✓	
May help with having fewer diaper rashes.	✓	

How to Tell If a Diaper Is the Right Size

Unlike baby clothes, disposable diapers are sized by a child's weight, not their age. Don't automatically assume a newborn baby is going to need a newborn diaper. If your baby is on the bigger side, a newborn diaper will wind up looking like a speedo on them. Follow the recommended size chart on the package to ensure the diaper size is right for your child's weight range. Before stocking up on diapers (which you're definitely going to need to do), buy a small pack first and make sure they fit.

> *TIP:*
> *Hold your baby while standing on a scale and check the weight. Then weigh yourself without your baby and calculate the difference. This is a quick method for finding out how much your baby weighs, if it's been a while since their last check-up.*

Just like grown-ups, baby bodies are unique, and since diaper brands are all different, you'll want to make sure the brand you have fits your baby comfortably. Even though diapers should fit snugly, there should also be some give. You should easily be able to put one finger in the waistband and two to three fingers between the diaper and your baby's leg. If the diaper is leaving red marks, it's probably either too tight or too small. And while leakage does happen, if it occurs often, that's also a sign that you probably need to change diaper sizes.

If you are going to use cloth diapers, they are available in "one size fits all" options that fit most babies from birth to potty training. Some also offer a variety of inserts so you can customize the absorbency depending on the age and size of your baby.

How to Change a Diaper

Needless to say, you'll be changing a lot of diapers. Your baby will probably cry or get fussy when they're ready for a new one, but there are other ways you can tell if they need a change too. Sometimes you'll see their face turn bright red as they grunt and strain while they poop. Don't worry if you miss the cue though. You'll probably smell it shortly after anyway. As for "number one" incidents, many disposable diapers come with color-changing stripes that alert you when they're wet. Before you start changing the diaper, make sure you're prepared with everything you need:

- **Diapers** – Obviously you'll need a clean one, but it's a good idea to have a spare one with you too if you're using disposables. Nothing is worse than being on your last one and having the fasten tabs rip.

- **Wipes** – Just like you don't want your only diaper to rip, you don't want to start changing a poopy diaper, only to find out there's only one wipe in the packet.

- **Spare Clothes** – Diapers can leak, so make sure you have spare clothes with you. Store a few next to your changing table and take a few changes of clothes when going out for extended periods of time.

- **Diaper Rash Cream** – You won't need it for every diaper change, but it's a good idea to have it on hand in case you do wind up needing it.

- **Blanket –** If you're changing your baby in a public restroom, or any place other than your regular changing table, you should put a protective cloth down for your baby to lie on. You could use a receiving blanket, swaddling blanket, or any other type of cloth big enough to cover the area.

- **Distractions** – While not a necessity, you may choose to have something with you to keep your baby distracted or entertained during diaper changes. Maybe a rattle, toy, pacifier, or something else that will keep their interest.

Now that you have everything you need, you're ready to change a diaper. Follow these easy steps:

1. If needed, place the protective blanket down where you will be changing your baby.

2. Place your baby on the changing table or surface where you will be changing them. Strap them in to minimize their movement and keep them from rolling around. While strapping your baby in will help keep them confined, it's not a guarantee they won't roll off the changing table, so never step away.

3. Check to see if you're dealing with a wet diaper or a soiled one. If you're not sure, gently pull the elastic around the back of the legs to peek inside.

4. Undo the pull tabs. If the diaper is soiled, take the front of the diaper and slide it down towards the baby's bottom to wipe away the majority of the waste. Then fold the diaper closed and rest the baby's bottom on the outside of the front of the diaper.

5. If you're changing a baby boy, immediately place a clean diaper or dry washcloth over the penis to protect you from getting sprayed. Keep the little squirt gun covered while you clean everything with wipes.

6. Clean the front area first and make sure to get all the folds and crevices.

   - **For Boys** – Don't forget to clean underneath the penis, and the scrotum. If your baby is uncircumcised, do not pull back the foreskin to clean underneath. If your baby was circumcised, the penis will take about a week to heal and will look red and possibly even scabby during this time. You may even see a bit of oozing or a small amount of blood, which is also normal. If any of these symptoms persist beyond a week, consult with your baby's doctor. When the area is clean, apply petroleum jelly over the tip of the penis after every diaper change to keep it from rubbing against the diaper and getting irritated.

- **For Girls** – Always wipe from front to back (from vulva to rectum) to prevent the spread of bacteria that can cause urinary tract infections. Do not pull the labia back to clean inside. Also, it's important to note that staying in a wet diaper for too long could cause pediatric vulvovaginitis, a condition that causes irritation and/or discharge in the area of the vulva and/or vagina. Monitoring and making diaper changes when necessary can help lessen your baby's risk of getting vulvovaginitis. If you notice any of these symptoms, contact your child's pediatrician.

7. After you've cleaned the front, lift the legs to clean the bottom area, remove the dirty diaper, and place a clean one under the baby's bottom.

8. Before fastening the new diaper, make sure the baby is completely dry and diaper rash cream or ointments were applied if needed. If the umbilical cord stump is still there, fold the top of the diaper down so it doesn't irritate it and to allow the stump to get air so it can heal. Also, if you have a boy, point his penis down before placing the diaper over it to prevent him from peeing out the top of his diaper.

9. Fasten the diaper and dispose of the dirty one in a diaper pail or garbage can.

10. Change your baby's clothes if needed. Check the sheet on the bed to see whether it needs to be changed too.

11. Wash your hands thoroughly when done. If you are away from home and don't have access to a sink, use antibacterial wipes or hand sanitizer if possible.

TIP:
Doggie poop bags are great for holding dirty diapers when you're away from home and can't find a trash can. They contain the mess and minimize the smell.

Swim Diapers

If your child is not potty trained, they're going to need swim diapers when they go swimming. Unlike regular diapers (which are super absorbent and would swell up like a balloon in the pool), swim diapers allow liquid to leak right through. This prevents the diaper from swelling up and becoming uncomfortable. But what's the point of a diaper if it just leaks everywhere?

Swim diapers are specifically designed to be worn in water. Their main purpose is to decrease the spread of fecal bacteria (like E. coli) that would contaminate public swimming areas. Notice I said "decrease" and not "prevent." Swim diapers can hold in some solid waste, but they will not prevent diarrhea from leaking through. If your child has diarrhea, they should stay out of the pool so they don't risk contaminating it and making others sick. If there's a "poop incident," the pool will have to be shut down for a couple of hours until it can be properly drained and cleaned. Don't be that parent who ruins the day for everyone else.

The Poop No One Warns You About

Babies ingest a lot of things while in utero such as amniotic fluid, bile, mucus, skin cells, and more. Their first bowel movement contains all of this in a nasty, greenish black tar substance called meconium. It's disgusting and extremely sticky, making it difficult to remove from your baby's skin. If you're lucky, a nurse will deal with this alien substance for you so you'll never even have to see it, although since it does take about a day or two to completely pass all of the meconium, there's still a chance you might encounter it. A trick is to lightly coat your newborn's skin with petroleum jelly or coconut oil for the first couple of days to prevent the meconium from sticking to it. This will make the first few diaper changes a lot easier.

Changing Tables

As mentioned earlier in this book, society is still catching up on modern-day parenting. The country is stuck in a belief that women should be the ones taking care of babies, which is why many places only have changing tables in women's restrooms. Things are slowly progressing, but in the meantime, what's a dad to do? Well, you can change your child on the restroom floor or counter, but those places are unsanitary and can pose health risks. You can carry spare blankets with you everywhere you go to cover surfaces in emergencies. You could also change your child in the backseat or trunk of your car (SUVs are awesome for this). Or, if you're dexterous, you can sit on a toilet seat, change your child on your lap, and pray you don't get anything on you. We're dads, though. We can do it! Where there's a will, there's a way. Check out these stories of dads dealing with public changing tables:

"It has been a challenge to find changing tables in public places. There have been times when we used changing tables in single-stalled women's bathrooms and had employees guard the door."
—Mike Degala

"My biggest pet peeve is changing tables. I'm flabbergasted at how many places don't take into consideration that dads can change diapers too! Whenever I come across a place like that, I make sure to talk to the manager and take it to the company's social media page."
—Chad Scanlon

"Looking back when our son was little, we took him to New York and went to some pretty fancy restaurants. One time, he needed his diaper changed and there were no changing stations in the men's restroom, so we changed him on the chair next to us. Needless to say it was a stink bomb of a poop, and we cleared the tables around us fairly quickly! We thought it was funny, the other patrons not so much!"
—BJ Barone

"We have had challenges with finding changing tables in public restrooms. We used to speak to a manager and complain if we had nowhere to change diapers. A fun story: We were invited to the White House for a Father's Day celebration when our son was an infant. His diaper needed to be changed, so we took him to the men's room, which is located in the White House Library. Upon finding no appropriate place to change his diaper, we went into the library and placed him on the bench in the room to change his diaper. We covered the bench with a changing pad so we would not have any accidents but were quickly notified that the bench was a historical piece and that since the entire space was a museum, we should be more careful. We were given a 'pass' once we exclaimed we had no other place to go to change him and were very careful."

—Tommy Starling

What to Do With an Explosive Poo

If you have an infant in diapers, the chances are that you'll probably have to deal with an explosive poo at some point. And when I say "explosive poo," I don't just mean a big, nasty, smelly diaper. I'm talking about a poop that can't be contained and basically explodes out of the diaper. You'll know it when you see it. In the case of an explosive poo, it manages to squeeze out of both leg openings and out the top of the diaper. It will go up the back and maybe even all the way up to the shoulder blades. Inside the diaper, it will be everywhere: front and back. It's basically a 360 degrees poo! And if your child sticks their hands in their diaper, well, lucky you. It will get all over their hands and everything they touch too.

It's terrifying when this happens, because shit is literally everywhere! If this happens to you, try to remain calm and just take your baby straight to the bathtub. There's no point in even trying to use wipes. They can't save you. Turn on the water, make sure it's lukewarm, and just rinse your child off. Wipe them down with a washcloth and make sure they are completely clean before drying them off and putting them in a new diaper and outfit. When they are clean, go back and assess the scene of the crime to make sure nothing else was contaminated. If poop got on anything else, make sure to clean it thoroughly, especially if it's something that would go in the baby's mouth, like a pacifier or teething ring. In those cases, if the items can be cleaned and sanitized in the dishwasher, make sure you do that. If not, consider throwing them away. For other items, like floors and baby gates, bleach wipes can sure come in handy.

REAL-LIFE STORY:

"While on parental leave with my son, if I didn't know what to do with my time, I'd often drive to Babies "R" Us. We'd always need something... diapers, formula, and on one occasion we were all out of portable diaper wipes. When we got there, he was hungry and needed a bottle, and they're cool with people using their glider chairs for feedings. Halfway through his bottle, his diaper exploded. Poop everywhere. Up his back. Out the sides. All over my left forearm. I had a change in the diaper bag... but I didn't have any wipes. And I couldn't put him down. We slowly made our way to the cash register, holding him with my left arm, pushing the cart and paying with my right." –Ian Hart

Doctors

Can a Doctor Legally Refuse to Care for You or Your Child Because of Your Sexual Orientation?

In 2015, national headlines were made after a pediatrician refused to treat the infant daughter of a legally married same-sex couple. Krista and Jami Contreras had carefully chosen Dr. Vesna Roi at Eastlake Pediatrics in Roseville, Michigan: a doctor who came highly recommended by their midwife. Dr. Roi knew they were lesbians, and after the first prenatal visit, they were under the impression that everything was fine. But the morning they arrived for the appointment, another pediatrician in the practice greeted them instead, explaining that Dr. Roi had a change of heart. After "much prayer," she decided that she couldn't treat their baby because they were lesbians. Guess what. Using "religious freedom" as an excuse to refuse treatment for a baby with same-sex parents was not illegal.

Even though the American Medical Association (AMA) and the American Academy of Pediatrics have ethics rules that prohibit discrimination based on sexual orientation and gender identity, these "rules" are only advisory. Some states have laws that prohibit doctors from discriminating against people based on their sexual orientation, but there are no federal laws that explicitly prohibit discrimination against LGBT individuals. This means in that in some states, doctors can legally refuse to treat a gay person, or their children, if they cite "religious freedom."

Finding LGBT-Friendly Doctors

How can you find a supportive doctor who will treat you and your children fairly, with understanding, compassion, and empathy? Insurance companies can typically help you find a doctor based on gender, practice, and location, but I have yet to find one that uses "LGBT friendly" as a sorting option. It's not that easy to find one online with this choice either.

GLMA (previously known as the Gay & Lesbian Medical Association) has a database of online medical professionals and is a good place to start, but their database is still growing so you may not be able to find an LGBT-friendly pediatrician near you when you search. Dr. Cattaneo says there are many other things you can do to help find an LGBT-friendly doctor for your child, though. Here are a few things he suggests:

- Ask for referrals from your local LGBT center or your local LGBT chamber of commerce if you have one.

- If there's an LGBT parenting group near you, ask the parents in that group if they have any recommendations.

- If you're able to do so, ask your birthmother or surrogate's obstetrician.

- Ask the nurses helping you during the delivery.

You can also interview doctors too. Call their offices beforehand and ask how comfortable they are treating a child with two gay dads. Have they done any special research about children of LGBT families? Do they have experience with children of LGBT families? Do they have anyone that can be a reference and tell you about their experience with the practice? Finally, while it's great that we support people and businesses that are "family," don't be afraid of going to a non-gay pediatrician. The most important thing is that you go for someone you can mesh with and have a comfortable relationship with.

Immunizations

To Vaccinate or Not to Vaccinate, That Is the Question

There are certain situations where some people can't get vaccinated because they're undergoing medical treatment or have a certain medical condition, but other than that, keeping your child up-to-date on recommended vaccinations is one of the best strategies to help keep them safe and healthy. Immunizations are the reason we don't see widespread epidemics of viruses and diseases like measles, polio, and smallpox. Some vaccines may cause side effects, such as fever, excessive sleepiness, and even seizures, but Dr. Cattaneo says the symptoms of the virus or bacteria can be much worse, so staying current with vaccinations is extremely important. Talk about vaccines with your pediatrician beforehand and discuss the possible side effects. You can also visit the Center for Disease Control and Prevention's website at www.cdc.gov for more information.

Don't Be the Odd One Out

It's important to remember that vaccines don't just protect the person being vaccinated: they protect the people around them too. So, in order to keep your child safe and healthy, it's important for you to be current on your immunizations as well. In fact, everyone that comes in contact with your child (grandparents, aunts, uncles, friends, neighbors, etc.) should all be current with their vaccinations, especially within the first few months of your baby's life. This is called cocooning because when everyone is vaccinated, they form a "cocoon" of disease protection around the baby.

But If Everyone Else is Immunized, Doesn't That Mean My Child Can't Get the Disease?

When a high percentage of the population is vaccinated and protected, it's difficult for a disease to spread because there are so few vulnerable people left to infect. This is called "herd immunity," but a high vaccination rate doesn't mean unvaccinated people are immune to getting sick.

Just look at the Eagle Mountain International Church in Newark, Texas.

In 2013, the vaccine-skeptical megachurch was linked to at least twenty-one cases of the measles. The majority of the people infected had not been immunized, making them susceptible to getting the disease.

Can Vaccines Cause Autism?

In 1998, Andrew Wakefield and twelve of his colleagues published a case series in the Lancet, which suggested a possible link between autism and the MMR (measles, mumps, rubella) vaccine. The paper received wide publicity, even though there was only a small sample size of twelve patients and there was no control group. It was later found out that Wakefield not only falsified the data, but he was also being funded by lawyers who had been engaged by parents in lawsuits against vaccine-producing companies. This was a major conflict of interest. Wakefield was eventually stripped of his medical license and ten of the original twelve authors of the study retracted their support. Years later, the Lancet retracted the study too. Other researchers could not replicate the original study, and the American Academy of Pediatrics has released numerous subsequent studies showing no link between vaccines and autism. Still, for some reason, the myth hasn't gone away.

Are There Benefits to Delayed Vaccination?

To ensure their safety, all vaccines go through extensive clinical trials for safety and efficacy before being licensed, and they are monitored constantly afterwards. If your child is healthy and has no medical reason to not receive an immunization, there is no benefit to a delayed vaccine schedule, according to Dr. Cattaneo. In fact, delaying vaccines can put a child at risk for illness. However, there could be medical reasons why a delayed schedule might be necessary. For example, a child receiving chemotherapy may not be able to receive immunizations at the "appropriate" times/intervals.

Vaccines in a Nutshell

Vaccines save lives. It's as simple as that. Get your kids vaccinated according to your doctors recommended schedule, and make sure you're up-to-date on your immunizations as well.

Traveling with
Children

Traveling is stressful, especially if it's your first time with a little one. Will you have trouble getting through airport security? Will your baby cry on the plane the whole time? Will your older child constantly kick the seat in front of them? How do you childproof a hotel? There's so much to think about, your head can spin—but with a little advanced planning, you can make things a whole lot easier for yourself, your child, and those around you. Here are a few tips for smooth traveling.

Infants and Toddlers

PACKING

If you're going to be traveling in a car or plane for a long time, strategically pack everything you need for the trip in a diaper bag and/or carry bag and keep it within arm's reach. If you're on a plane, your bag should go under the seat in front of you and not in the overhead bin. That way, you can access it during takeoff, landing, and any other time you're not permitted to get out of your seat.

The more organized your bag is, the easier it's going to be for you to access things quickly when you need them. Trust me, when you have a hungry, screaming baby on your lap in the plane, the last thing you're going to want to do is fumble around in a diaper bag trying to find a bottle, formula, and burp cloth. To make things easier on yourself, keep everything you need for diaper changes in one section, everything you need for feeding (bottles, formula, burp cloth) in another section, and distraction toys in another. Make sure the things you will need most are easy to grab, not at the bottom of the bag where you have to dig for them. If your child uses pacifiers, keep a few of them in a side pocket for easy access. Also, make sure you pack a change of clothes in your carry-on for yourself too in case you get puked, peed, or pooped on.

TIP:

Consider using Ziploc bags to create multiple changing packs and fill each of them with a diaper and a change of clothes. When changing your baby, if the clothes are wet or soiled and need to be changed, you can seal the dirty outfit in the Ziploc before putting it back in your diaper bag.

AIRPORT SECURITY

Going through airport security with an infant or toddler for the first time can be a challenge. In addition to holding your little one, you also have to get your bags in the bins, take out your laptops, and remove your shoes, belts, etc. There are a few things you can do though to make the process easier for you.

1. Make sure you have the right documents with you: either a copy of your child's birth certificate or an adoption document. The TSA agent may not always ask for this when you go through security, but if you look different from your child or have different last names, you may wind up having issues. It's best to always err on the side of caution.

2. If you have an infant, consider using a baby carrier to strap them to your chest when going through security. Not only will this free up your hands so you can manage your carry-ons, but many TSA agents (if you ask them nicely) will let you walk right through the metal detectors with these on too. This is

great, especially if your child is sleeping, because you won't have to wake them up when going through security. Strollers on the other hand, must be screened by X-ray. So, if you're in the security line and your child is asleep in the stroller, you risk waking them up when you have to take them out.

3. You can bring liquid and powdered formula through security, but you should let the agent know you have formula before it goes through the X-ray machine. If you don't want it to go through the X-ray, let them know so they can do alternative screening methods.

SURVIVING FLIGHTS

When people seated on the airplane see you walking down the aisle with a baby, they're probably secretly praying that you keep walking past them. Everyone assumes that babies are going to cry on airplanes. No one likes sitting next to a screaming baby, and let's face it, no parent wants their child to be the one screaming on the plane either. While there's nothing you can do to guarantee your child won't cry on the plane, there are definitely steps you can take to minimize the likelihood. Here are a few things you can try.

1. **Feed During Takeoff and Landing** – The pressure in the plane changes during takeoff and landing and the pressure will hurt your little one's ears. The pressure can make infants scream uncontrollably. Feeding from a bottle can release pressure and basically does the same thing for infants that chewing gum does for adults, so time your feeding to coincide with takeoff and landing. A pacifier may also work because of the sucking motion, but

feeding will calm a baby more and possibly even help them fall asleep.

2. **Coordinate Nap Time** – If you can coordinate it so that your child sleeps on the plane, you're in luck! If they're getting sleepy and you don't board for another twenty minutes or so, try to keep them awake until you can give them a bottle during takeoff. Hopefully they'll drift off to sleep then. Of course, there is no guarantee they will sleep on the plane, but whatever you can do to help make it happen will make things easier for you.

3. **Keep Plane Toys Separate** – Keep two sets of toys with you: a couple of toys to play with in the airport, and a couple that only come out during the plane ride. Babies lose interest in things quickly. Reserving a couple of toys for in-flight play only will hopefully keep them amused longer.

4. **Good Toys vs. Bad Toys** – You're going to be in a confined space, so choose toys wisely. Small cars, trucks, planes, or basically anything with wheels can easily fall on the ground and roll under the seat. They can even roll down the aisle and into other rows. Wheels are definitely a no-no. If your child is old enough to color, consider buying triangular shaped crayons. They're bulky, so they're easy for kids to hold and you don't have to worry about them rolling off the tray. Also, no-mess-markers are great because they only color the special paper they come with, so you don't have to worry about your child coloring the trays or seats.

5. **iPads, Tablets, and Phones** – Consider downloading a few age-appropriate games for the flight to keep your little one entertained. Keep in mind that some games require an Internet connection and your

plane may or may not have Internet capabilities. Consider downloading a few non-Internet games just to be safe.

6. **Be Creative** – Infants and toddlers can be amused by almost anything. When they've lost interest in their toys, see what other things you can do to keep them entertained. Maybe they can play with the plastic cups your drinks come in, or maybe they can play with your keys.

STAYING IN HOTELS

Hotels can be rough for little ones. Your child will be in an unfamiliar place so they may not feel as comfortable or secure as they do at home. Also, they will be in a confined space without a lot of room to run around, so they may get antsy. Stress can build up quickly, but there are a few things you can do to help make your stay more comfortable.

1. When making your hotel reservation, check to see what they can do to help accommodate small children. They may be able to provide things like a Pack 'n Play, crib, and high chair. They may even be able to childproof the room before your arrival.

2. Decide whether you would like to be near or far away from the elevators. Being closer to the elevator means you are in and out faster and won't have to haul your luggage very far. The downside is that everyone on that floor will need to use the elevator, so the closer you are, the nosier it might be. If noise is a concern, you can also ask if you can get a room far away from other guests.

3. While your home may be babyproofed to the nines, hotels are another matter entirely. Not only are

there safety hazards around every corner, there are also germs everywhere! How many people have touched that TV remote, and what were they doing beforehand? Chances are, it wasn't washing their hands. Here are a few suggestions for making sure your child stays as safe and germ-free as possible (you'll notice quickly that tape is your best friend). These are only suggestions, so do whatever you're comfortable with.

- When making your reservation, check to see whether the hotel has the ability to childproof the room.

- Put duct tape over any exposed electrical outlet. Make sure not to get the tape on the walls, because it can peel off the paint or wallpaper.

- Identify all the things you don't want your child to play with and move those items somewhere (like the top shelf of the closet) where they can't be reached. If they won't fit, call the front desk or housekeeping and ask if they will remove the items. Things to consider moving include alarm clocks, coffee makers, hair dryers, pens, books, magazines, baskets of snacks, phones, trashcans, etc.

- Tape cabinets and drawers closed so that your children cannot rummage through them or pinch their fingers in them. Remember, duct tape can remove paint and may even damage drawers, so use something like a painters tape for this.

- If there's a mini-fridge in the room that doesn't require a key to open, consider taping it shut too. Your little one doesn't need that bottle of rum, and you don't want to have to pay for it either.

- Jiggle the TV a bit to make sure it's secure. If it wobbles too much, push it back out of reach or put it on the floor so it doesn't accidentally fall on your child. Also, make sure the remote is out of reach. If you are OK with your child playing with the remote, consider wiping it down first. Those things are germ-infested.

- Make sure all windows and doors are locked. Make sure you also deadbolt the main door in case your child is able to open the door with the handle.

- If the curtains have pull cords, tape them up out of reach.

- If there are loose electrical cords, tape them back behind furniture.

- If there's an air-conditioning/heating unit on the floor with access to the controls, cover it with tape.

- Tape washcloths over sharp edges on furniture to prevent your little ones from hitting their heads on them.

- Move soaps, shampoo, lotions, and all other toiletries out of reach.

- Tape the toilet seat down to prevent your child from playing in the water and/or smashing their fingers under the seat.

These are just a few suggestions for making your room safer for children. Different hotel rooms may have different types of dangers, so it's important to do what you feel is necessary based on your environment. And of course, nothing is better than adult supervision, because no matter what lengths we take to secure the area, children are bound to find something we miss.

School-Aged Children

Traveling with school-aged children is completely different than traveling with infants and toddlers. They are more mobile and often able to entertain themselves. Still, they can get bored easily and may not have a lot of patience for long lines or waiting periods. Here are a few things you can do to make trips with school-aged children easier.

PACKING

Since younger children can go through a range of emotions, understanding these emotions and packing accordingly can go a long way. Think about things you can pack to help counter boredom, overexcitement, tiredness, and more.

- If your child is going to be sitting still for long periods of time (in the airport lounge, plane seat, car, etc.), consider letting your child pick entertainment kits, like coloring books and crayons or activity and puzzle books.

- Handheld game devices can keep your children entertained for hours.

- Download games and/or activities for your tablet or iPad if you have one. There are many educational apps disguised as games, so you don't have to feel guilty letting your child play on the device for long periods of time.

- Pack a set of headphones. This will allow your children to watch movies, listen to music, and play their noisy games without disturbing other passengers.

- Have plenty of snacks available to keep your kids from getting hungry and cranky.

- In case your child gets overexcited to the point where they're basically bouncing off the walls, pack something basic to help channel that energy. Maybe they could use a pen and paper to make a list of things they want to do on the trip, or maybe they could keep a journal to remember everything that happens along the way. Another option is to bring a map and have your child locate where you currently are and the places you will go. Talk about things like what you'll see on the trip and how far away the destination is.

AIRPORT SECURITY

Just like traveling with an infant or toddler, you'll want to make sure you have the right documents with you: either a copy of your child's birth certificate or an adoption document. The TSA agent may not always ask for this when you go through security, but if you look different from your child or have different last names, you may wind up having issues. It's best to always err on the side of caution.

If your child can walk on their own, getting though airport security should be easier. Depending on their age, they may be able to leave their shoes on and go through the metal detector as opposed to being screened through the Advanced Imaging Technology. One parent (sometimes both if the agent allows) can go through the metal detector immediately after their child.

If your child has a disability, medical condition, or medical device, mention this to the TSA agent so you can determine the best way to get them through security. Your child should not have to get out of a wheelchair or any other mobility device if they use one.

SURVIVING FLIGHTS

Long flights can be hard for children who don't like being confined in small spaces for extended periods of time. A little preparation can go a long way when it comes to helping your child get through this experience. Try some of these ideas.

- **Snacks** – Have plenty of snacks available. You never know when your child will get hungry, and it may be a while until a flight attendant will offer food.

- **Keep Plane Toys Separate** – Just like with infants and toddlers, school-aged children can get bored with toys and activities quickly. Consider keeping aside a couple of toys and/or activities for when you are actually in the plane. This could help make the flight more special for them and more bearable for you.

- **Good Toys vs. Bad Toys** – Again, just like with toddlers and infants, avoid things that can roll away (cars, crayons, etc.) if they fall off of the tray and onto the floor. Triangular crayons are great because they can't roll. Also avoid noisy toys unless your child can use headphones with them. Good toys at this age are handheld games, tablets, coloring and activity books, reading books, etc...

- **iPads, Tablets, and Phones** – Consider downloading a few age-appropriate games for the flight to keep your little one entertained. Keep in mind that some games require an Internet connection and your plane may or may not have Internet capabilities. Consider downloading a few non-Internet games just to be safe. Don't forget the headphones.

STAYING IN HOTELS

While you won't need to go through extensive childproofing like you do for infants and toddlers, there are still a few things you may want to consider. Parental controls are available on the TV to prevent your child from accidentally (or intentionally) stumbling across inappropriate channels. Also, keep in mind that some actions, such as removing items from the mini-fridge or making phone calls, may automatically put charges on rooms. Make sure your children know the rules for what they can and cannot touch and remove anything you have concerns with. Also, make sure all doors and windows are securely locked.

Childproofing Round One – The Early Years

Babies are constantly putting themselves in harm's way. Seriously, if there's anything dangerous around, your fearless, curious, death-defying stunt child will definitely find it. Luckily, most accidents are preventable, and there are lots of things you can do to keep your child safe. Below is a checklist for steps you can take to minimize the risk of an unexpected trip to the emergency room.

Basic Childproofing Checklist

Sleeping Area – Keep your baby's crib free of pillows, bumpers, stuffed animals, loose fitted sheets, and blankets. Your baby should be sleeping prison-style. All they get is a mattress and a fitted sheet. To keep them warm throughout the night, have them wear a sleep sack. Do not let your baby sleep overnight while swaddled. A swaddling blanket that comes unwrapped could cover your baby's face and increase the risk of suffocation. Also, make sure the mattress is on the lowest position to lessen the chance of them climbing out. Make sure your baby's crib is not next to a window, heating vent, or radiator. All loose items, such as toys, baby monitors, electrical cords, cords on the window blinds, etc. should be at least three feet away from the crib.

Doors – Secure all knobs on doors that go to off-limit areas such as the basement, garage, and outside. Consider getting doorstops or door holders if you are concerned about your child getting their fingers or hands caught in closing doors or door hinges. Also, regarding those little springy doorstoppers that prevent doors from slamming into walls: it's recommended that you glue the tips of them on or get the one-piece stoppers so that your child doesn't take off the tips and put them in their mouth.

Windows – Secure all windows by installing locking devices. Make sure you can still open them in case of an emergency, such as a fire.

Window Treatments – If you have window coverings with cords, make sure the cords are out of your child's reach at all times. Wrap them around hooks or get blind cord winders.

Electrical Cords and Outlets – Hide all electrical cords behind furniture if possible, to prevent your baby from chewing or playing with them. Tape or fasten them to a wall or floor if necessary. Make sure all electrical outlets are also covered, and don't keep lamps in places where your child can touch hot bulbs.

Stairs – Install baby gates on every stair access point, and anywhere else you want to keep off limits.

Balconies and Railings – Keep couches, chairs, and other furniture away from balconies and railings to prevent children from climbing over them. If you have posts or railings that are more than three inches apart, consider getting a mesh wall or another type of temporary barrier to prevent your little one from sliding through and/or getting stuck.

Furniture – Anchor TVs, dressers, bookcases, lamps, and any other type of furniture that could tip over.

Toy Boxes – Open shelves and bins are safer than chests; however, if you plan on using a chest around the house, make sure it has a lightweight lid that won't slam shut on your child's fingers. There should also be small air holes in case your little one climbs in.

Choking Hazards – Small items that can fit in your child's mouth should be kept out of reach. This includes loose change, marbles, stones, jewelry, hard candies, and other small objects.

Batteries – Batteries contain hazardous chemicals and can be extremely dangerous if swallowed. Fully-charged batteries should be securely stored. Dead batteries should be properly disposed of immediately after being removed.

Miscellaneous Items – Put breakables, valuables, and other off-limit items on high shelves out of reach, or store them in another location.

Plants – Keep plants out of reach, and make sure there are no poisonous ones inside or outside of your house. A quick search online can help you determine whether the plants you have are poisonous. If you're still not sure, replace them.

Fire Safety – Install smoke alarms and carbon monoxide detectors throughout your house and check them every month. Also, fireplaces, heaters, furnaces, and radiators should have protective barriers to keep children from burning themselves. Matches, lighters, and anything else that can start a fire should be secured.

Cleaning Supplies – House cleaners like bleach, glass cleaners, wood polishers, dishwashing tablets, and laundry detergents should be up high and out of reach. Pesticides and other chemicals should be stored out of reach too. You might even want to keep them in secured cabinets.

Plastic Bags – If you keep plastic bags in the house, make sure they are stored out of reach. Any other plastic bag that comes into the house (dry cleaning bags, produce bags, plastic wrapping, etc.) should be disposed of immediately.

Pets – Cats like to curl up to warm things, and they may try to snuggle with your sleeping baby. This is dangerous for many reasons. Cats could bite, scratch, or even smother your baby. To train cats to stay away from the crib, cover a large piece of cardboard in aluminum foil and place it over the crib mattress (when your baby is not in it, of course). Cats hate the crinkling sound and after placing them on the cover, hopefully they will avoid the crib from that point forward. If aluminum foil doesn't work, try covering the cardboard with double-sided sticky tape. Cats don't like sticky paws either. Other pet-related things to consider include keeping dog and cat food bowls in separate areas to prevent your child from getting in the food or water, and making sure litter boxes are in separate areas too. You definitely don't want your child playing in a poop-filled sandbox.

Workout Equipment – Lots of people have workout equipment in their homes, and while they may not look dangerous, chances are that they most certainly are. Treadmills, exercise bikes, elliptical machines, and other equipment have various places that can pinch fingers, bump heads, and more. Treadmills also have safety cords that can shut a machine off in an emergency, but those cords can pose a strangulation risk for your child. Children should be kept away from exercise equipment at all times. If you don't have a dedicated room where the equipment can be locked away, use baby gates to section them off. If your child has to be in the same room as you while you work out, keep them in another area of the room away from the equipment, but in a place where they are still visible.

DID YOU KNOW?

In 2009, Mike Tyson's four-year-old daughter was injured in a treadmill accident at his home. A cable that was attached to the exercise machine had wrapped around her neck and strangled her. After freeing her from the cord, her mother called 911 and started CPR, but unfortunately it was too late. She eventually died in the hospital. Many people don't realize how dangerous exercise equipment can be for young children, but injuries from them are common and children should be kept away from exercise equipment at all times.

Pools – Fence off pools and hot tubs if you have them. Also, install a pool alarm, a device that alerts you when someone disturbs the surface of the pool, opens a gate to the pool, or removes a cover.

Firearms - Keep guns unloaded and locked away. Store bullets in a separate locked location.

The Kitchen

Sharp Objects – Knives, scissors, letter openers, sharp kitchen utensils, and other pointy objects should be secured in drawers that can't open.

Cling Wrap and Tin Foil – Plastic cling wrap and tin foil boxes have sharp cutting edges that can be dangerous. They should be kept out of reach of children.

Trashcans – It's a good idea to only use trashcans and recycling containers that have lids. Otherwise your curious child may decide to sample some new bacteria. They may also decide to make lovely new messes.

Sponges – These are bacteria cesspools and can make your child very sick. Plus, they are major choking hazards if a piece is bitten off. Keep sponges out of reach.

Stoves and Ovens – Install stove-knob covers on your burner controls. Also, appliance latches can be used to prevent your little one from opening conventional and microwave ovens.

Refrigerator – Keep your child out of the fridge by installing an appliance latch. Also, magnets are dangerous if swallowed. If you feel like you need to have them on the fridge, make sure they are larger in size (to lessen the chance of them being swallowed) and kept high enough that they are out of reach.

Appliances - Keep all items away from the edges of tables and countertops. This includes things like toasters, mixers, juicers, blenders, knife blocks, etc.

Dishwasher – Install an appliance latch so your child doesn't open the dishwasher and reach for something sharp or breakable. Also, remember to keep the detergent locked away.

The Bathroom

Doors – Make sure you install doorknob covers to prevent your child from closing the door and locking themselves in.

Toiletries – Colognes, perfumes, cosmetics, mouthwashes, toothpaste, skincare, hair products, and other toiletries can be toxic. They should be secured.

Medications – Prescriptions, medicines, vitamins, supplements, and anything else that can be potentially harmful if swallowed should be locked away. Yes, Viagra and PrEP too, so if you have anything bedside, make sure it's secured. While you're at it, if you have Viagra or PrEP, check the expiration dates because if you have an infant in the house, chances are you're not using them very often anymore.

Cabinets – Install cabinet locks to keep your child from getting into any contents you don't want them getting into.

Toilets – Install a lid lock to prevent your child from slamming the lid on their fingers or turning your toilet into a new splash pool. Also, children can drown in just a couple of inches of water, so unlocked toilets are drowning risks.

Hair Dryers – These can easily be knocked into the sink, bathtub, or toilet, and the cord could also get wrapped around your child's neck. Keep hair dryers out of reach.

Sharp Objects – Razors should not be kept on tubs or on sink counters. Make sure razors, tweezers, scissors, nail clippers, and any other sharp grooming objects are secured out of reach.

Bathtub – Install a faucet shield to protect your child from hitting their head on the faucet. Remember to never leave your child alone in the bath, not even for a second, and always drain the tub after use.

Water Temperature – Set the max water temperature in your home to 120 degrees to minimize the chance of accidental scalding. If you are unable to set the water temperature in your home, consider installing a scald guard which will slow the water flow if it reaches a temperature that is too high.

Bath Rugs – Use nonskid rugs to help prevent slips and falls. Also, consider getting a rubber bath mat for inside the tub.

Home Office

Computer Monitor – If you have a desktop monitor, make sure it's far away from the edge of your desk and consider bolting it down so your little one doesn't pull it on top of themself.

Choking Hazards – Make sure your desk remains tidy and there are no small items that your child can put in their mouth and choke on. This includes rubber bands, paper clips, pen caps, and things often found on desks and work spaces.

Electrical Cords and Outlets – If you have a lot of cords running into one outlet, consider threading them through a tube to prevent your baby from chewing or playing with them. Also use a surge protector cover.

Bookcases – Make sure all bookcases are anchored to the wall so your child doesn't pull them on top of themselves and get pinned down or hurt.

Childproofing Your Home Can Be Fabulous!

Baby-proofing products are not known for being particularly stylish, and let's face it—many of them can be downright hideous. They can be obtrusive or gaudy, and they can even clash with your home décor, but here's a little secret: it doesn't have to be that way! You don't have to stick foam corners on everything in your house in order to keep your child safe. With a little effort, it's possible to childproof your home in a way that doesn't cramp your style. Here are a few options that allow you to make your home safe while keeping it fashionable in the process.

Baby Gates – Most gates are made out of metal, mesh, or wood and stand out like a sore thumb. With a little effort though, you can find designer ones that are modern, elegant, and stylish. There are options for clamping around banisters and spindles instead of drilling into them, and you can even have fireplace gates stained to match your mantle or floor. There are retractable options too, so that the gate hides when it's not in use. Be creative! Try searching online for "stylish," "modern," "decorative," and "customized" baby gates to get a few ideas.

Electrical Outlet Covers – There are many options when it comes to childproofing electrical outlets. You can opt for the cheap option where you plug a small cover into the actual outlet, but these can be a pain to remove every time you need to plug something in. Also, if your child pulls a cord out from the wall, you now have an exposed outlet for them to stick their little fingers in. Look for options that cover the entire outlet and require you to slide or swivel the cover when plugging something in. When you remove a plug from these, they automatically slide shut. These types of electrical outlets offer more protection, they look better, and they're fairly inexpensive too.

Stove Knob Covers – You can find cheap options that are clear and don't make it difficult for adults to access. If you are going to be looking for new appliances in the near future, consider getting a cooktop with the knobs on top. They're modern and stylish, and the knobs are placed in a position that is more difficult for a child to reach.

Cabinets and Drawers – You're going to need to lock away those sharp knives and other dangerous things hidden in drawers and cabinets. Unfortunately, the majority of locks out there are bulky and just plain ugly! If you're looking for something that won't be an eyesore, consider magnetic locks or similar concealed locks that are easy to use and won't compromise the visual aesthetic of your home.

Coffee Tables – Hard and pointed edges on coffee tables can be major hazards for children because they're just the right height for toddlers to hit their heads when they fall. Consider getting a circular table without corners or a large ottoman that's soft and easy to clean. For ottomans, you can place a tray on top whenever you need a temporary sturdy surface for drinks or food. If you have tables with corners and you don't want to remove them, you can always get clear corner protectors.

Rugs and Carpet Tiles – If you have hardwood or tiled floors, you can create a stylish soft spot for your child with cute rugs or carpet tiles. They come in various styles, colors, and patterns, so you can find one that matches your décor.

Blind Cord Winders – If you have blinds on your windows, it's important that you secure the cords and keep them away from your little one. Blind cord winders allow you to wrap up loose cords and keep them securely out of reach. They're available in different colors to match your blinds and blend in.

Break-Resistant Glasses – Acrylic stemware and barware allows you to have nice glasses without the worry of having them shatter. They can look just like glass and are great for indoor and outdoor parties.

Picture Frames – Opt for picture frames with acrylic instead of glass. That way if your child gets ahold of the picture and drops it, you don't have to worry about pieces of shattered glass going everywhere.

Flameless Candles – If you love candles, don't worry. You don't have to live without them in order to keep your baby safe. Battery-operated, flameless candles are available in various different sizes, from pillars to votives and tea lights. Some create a nice glow, while others have flickering options to give the sense of a real flame. There are even scented options. Some are more realistic than others, so look around until you find something that you like.

Getting Professional Help

Childproofing a home can be overwhelming. If you don't have the time, or if you're afraid you might miss something, you might want to consider hiring a professional childproofing service. There are companies that will assess your home and address safety concerns accordingly. They can install gates and window guards, secure furniture and doors, and address any other risks. They can even safeguard your pool if you have one. It's not a cheap service, but if you're worried you might miss something, it could give you peace of mind. The International Association for Child Safety (IAFCS) can help you find childproofing services. Their website is www.iafcs.org. You could also do a general search online for childproofing services. Just make sure you check references and reviews.

Early Bonding with Your Children

Regardless if you are welcoming an infant or an older child into your family, early bonding with them is going to be extremely important. There are various types of bonding activities that you can do based on age level and background. Here are a few examples:

Bonding with Infants and Toddlers

SKIN-TO-SKIN CONTACT

Skin-to-skin contact, sometimes referred to as Kangaroo Care, is a wonderful way to bond with infants. It's simple and easy to do, especially during feeding and nap times. Just remove your shirt and your baby's clothes (except for their diaper), and hold your baby so that the two of you are skin-to-skin. For naps, hold your baby so you are chest-to-chest. Then place a blanket over your child without covering their face and…voilà! You instantly become a human incubator. There are numerous benefits to skin-to-skin contact including:

- **Enhanced Bonding** – Remember when we talked about oxytocin in the "Things About Parenthood No One Tells You About" section? It's that important attachment/bonding chemical that's released when you spend time with your child. Every time you experience skin-to-skin contact with your baby, your body releases oxytocin and enables that initial connection to occur naturally.

- **Regulating Your Baby's Body** – Your body can help regulate your baby's body temperature, and when you are chest-to-chest, your body can help regulate your baby's heart rate and breathing too.

- **Baby Cries Less** – The rhythm of your heart in conjunction with your warm body can help calm your baby, making them cry less.

- **Better Sleep for Your Baby and Less Stress for Everyone** – Since skin-to-skin contact can help keep your baby calm, it will likely be easier for them to fall asleep. Having a baby that sleeps more and cries less can also help keep you in a more calm and relaxed state. Well, as much as you can be with an infant in the house.

- **Better Growth and Development** – A calm baby that cries less and sleeps more can spend more time taking everything in, thus devoting more time to growth and development, both physically and mentally.

Even though feeding and nap times are perfect occasions for skin-to-skin contact, there are plenty of other opportunities for it as well. You can pretty much practice it anytime you're holding your baby, well anywhere it's appropriate for you to walk around shirtless.

EYE CONTACT

Another important factor of bonding is eye contact. Babies thrive off of it. Newborns are nearsighted for the first few months of their lives, so you'll have to be within eight to fifteen inches from their face while practicing eye contact. If you hold your infant in your arms during feeding times, your face will be the perfect distance, and when you lock eyes while practicing skin-to-skin contact during feeding times, you're basically emulating rock-star parenting skills!

OTHER PHYSICAL CONTACT

Babies love interaction, and there are many bonding techniques you can do with physical touch. Here are a few examples:

- **Kissing** – Kiss them on their foreheads, cheeks, hands, and feet.

- **Hand Grips** – Let your child grip one of your fingers. While they're holding on, try different types of interactions, such as slowly moving your hands in circles or tapping their hands with your thumb.

- **Apply Lotion** – A gentle massage can be calming for your baby. When using lotion, steer clear of ones that use perfume or dyes.

RESPONDING TO CRIES

Some people say that parents should allow their children to cry before responding to their needs, but it's important to keep in mind that infants are only able to express their needs through crying. When they cry, they are trying to tell you something (they're hungry, they're tired, they need a change, etc.). Quickly responding to an infant's cries can help build trust. In the beginning, try responding to their cries within thirty seconds and scale back in response time as they get older.

BABY CARRIERS

Carrying your baby or toddler against your chest via a carrier has many benefits. Not only does it free up your hands, but it strengthens the bond between you and your child since it allows you to stay close throughout the day. Your heartbeat and breathing patterns can also help keep your child in a calmer state, and you don't have to worry about maneuvering a stroller when you're out and about.

Bonding with Older Children

If you are expanding your family by welcoming an older child into your home, your bonding experience is going to be completely different than if you were welcoming a newborn. First of all, there are likely going to be trust issues that need to be overcome. Whatever living situation your child was in beforehand didn't work out, and they may be afraid that living with you isn't going to work out either. Your child may have had numerous placements before finding you, and they may be wondering how long it's going to be until they have to move on to another family. You're going to need to find a way to build trust and form a meaningful bond. This can take a long time, so patience and perseverance are key.

Also, keep in mind that children often wind up in foster care as a result of neglect, abuse, divorce, the death of a legal guardian, or various other unfortunate events that could disrupt a home. Every child's background and history is different, so what works for bonding with one child may not work for another. For example, a normal bedtime routine might include tucking a child into bed and giving them a hug and kiss goodnight, but that could be traumatizing for a child with a history of sexual abuse. Remember, social workers are there to help, so ask them for tips and ideas for what kind of bonding exercises might work for your family. You'll find a few examples below that may work for various ages. Periodically check in with your social worker to give updates and ask about different types of bonding exercises if the ones you are using don't seem to be working.

GETTING COMFORTABLE

Get on the Same Level – Some kids may not want to interact right away. If this is the case, you can still bond by being at the same level and sharing interests in close proximity to each other. For example, if your child is sitting and coloring at the table, you can sit next to them at the table and color too. If they are lying on the floor reading a book, you can lie on the floor and quietly read a book next to them. You don't have to interact or speak with each other, but you can get comfortable with being in the same space with each other while doing the same kind of activities.

ENCOURAGING EYE CONTACT

Use a Sticker – Without your child noticing, place a sticker on your face right between your eyes. Don't say anything about it and see how long it takes for them to notice.

Follow an Object – Play a game where your child has to keep their eyes on an object in your hand. Slowly move the object side to side, up and down, in a figure eight, and basically all over the place. Every few seconds, stop the object between your eyes so that your child looks at you for a couple of seconds before moving it again.

Peek-a-Boo – If your child has trouble making eye contact, you might be able to slowly work on it by playing a game of "Peek-a-Boo." It doesn't have to be covering your eyes with your hands like you would with a baby, but you could playfully peek around a corner and say, "I see you," before hiding again.

ENCOURAGING PHYSICAL CONTACT

Brush, Comb, or Braid Hair – It sounds simple, but brushing, combing, and braiding hair allows you to spend time with your child and have physical contact with them in a non-threatening way. Depending on the comfort and trust levels, you can do this in silence, hum or sing a song, or have conversations while brushing hair.

Painting Nails – Painting your child's fingernails and toenails can introduce physical contact and allow children to express themselves artistically at the same time. In addition to different paint colors, you can also use stickers and gems if you want to get fancy. And if your inner drag persona wants to express herself too, maybe your child can even paint your nails. Make sure you have nail polish remover on hand if you are concerned about looking too fabulous outside of the house.

Play Hand Games – Paper, Rock, Scissors, Patty Cake, and Thumb Wars are examples of games that involve non-threatening physical contact.

Three-Legged Race – It doesn't necessarily have to be a race. You could even try tying one of your legs to one of your child's legs and just walking around the house. This game involves physical contact and also encourages communication and teamwork.

ENHANCING COMMUNICATION AND INTERACTION

Read a Story – You can read a story to your child, or you can read together. This is a great bonding exercise because you can sit next to each other and increase vocabulary skills, literacy, critical thinking, and imagination.

Play Leader-Follower Games – There are many games that can be used to enhance communication and build trust at the same time. For example, "Red Light, Green Light" and "Simon Says" both involve people following someone's lead. "Mother May I" is also a great example too, although you may want to consider calling it "Father May I." It's completely up to you.

Play Ball – A simple back and forth game can be played with various types of coordination levels. You could roll a ball back and forth for younger kids. For older kids, you could kick a soccer ball back and forth or play a game of catch. A game of "Hot Potato" could also work for a child who has more energy.

Projects – Do a project together that involves working together physically to achieve a goal. Maybe complete a puzzle or build a model car.

Parenting Groups

Parenting groups can be extremely helpful for new parents. They're an opportunity for your kids to meet and play with other children; they give you an opportunity to get advice from others who are at the same stage of parenting as you; and they give you a chance to actually talk to other adults (something necessary for all new stay-at-home dads cooped up with someone who only knows how to say goo goo gaa gaa). But unfortunately, parenting groups can be a bit hit-or-miss for gay dads.

Many parenting groups are catered towards stay-at-home moms, because women have traditionally been the stay-at-home caregivers, and the groups give them an opportunity to hang out with other moms. This is blatantly obvious because many of the parenting groups reference mothers only, like "Mom's Day Out," or "Moms and Tots" or something along those lines. Sometimes, men are not welcomed into the group at all. Other times, they may make an exception for gay dads because they consider a gay man to be "one of the girls." Or maybe they've gotten past the whole gender-roles thing and accept parents regardless of gender.

There might also be an LGBT parenting group in your area, which is awesome if it's relatively close to you. Unfortunately, because there aren't as many LGBT parents as straight parents, there aren't as many local LGBT parenting groups either. You may find that you have to travel quite a distance to get to a play date or picnic, which isn't something that's sustainable in the long run when we all have busy lives. If you can though, try to get to an LGBT parenting group meeting a few times while your child is young so they can see other kids with same-gender parents. You can search for "LGBT Parenting Groups" plus your city and state to see if there's one near you. The Family Equality Council is also a great resource. Check them out at www.familyequality.org.

Finally, if you can't find an LGBT parenting group to attend in person, try looking for online parenting groups. They're great for getting advice from other gay dads, and you don't have to travel anywhere. Here are a few Facebook groups you may want to join.

Gay Fathers:
www.facebook.com/groups/15368945293/

Gay Dads
www.facebook.com/groups/7181147876/

LGBTQ + Parenting:
www.facebook.com/groups/1665204943700662/

Honestly parenting groups are a mixed bag. You may have bad experiences with them, you may have wonderful experiences with them, you may decide to skip them all together, or you may decide to create your own. To see what I mean, here are a few experiences other gay dads have had with parenting groups:

"We were not allowed to join our neighborhood mothers group. It would not have been much of an issue, except that one of my friends started the group (before we moved to the neighborhood). It got weirder because we've twice accidentally found ourselves at their Halloween party at the local playground, and our son is close friends with a number of the kids. He crashed the party. Somewhat awkward for the parents. Not for the kids. After several years we got an invite to their Easter Egg Hunt, but declined. The damage was done."
—Ian Hart

"There were many baby groups we attended that were specifically called 'Moms and Tots.' When suggested that they should change the name of the group they said, 'Well it's mostly mothers who attend the classes.'"
—**BJ Barone**

"We live in a very gay friendly area of the nation but there aren't that many gay parents (yet). I find playgroups and parenting groups to be one of the most discriminatory things I've faced. I'm a stay-at-home dad and have faced having to be approved by other moms on a regular basis, I've actually given up trying to expand my circle because it is exhausting having to be 'vetted' just to attend a play date. On a positive note, we have an 'all-gay' parents group that gets together monthly."
—**Chad Scanlon**

"An important factor for us has been our involvement with Modern Family Alliance, a local volunteer organization that hosts social gatherings and educational events for LGBT families. These gatherings gave our son the opportunity to meet and play with other kids who are part of non-traditional families."
—**Michael Hadley**

"Find other gay dads in your community. I never realized how many gay men have adopted in our area, until we started connecting on Facebook via foster/adoption pages in our area. They are great resource. Everyone parents differently, and you can all learn something from one another."
—**Adam White**

Questions You
Might Get Asked
and How to
Respond to Them

Knock, knock.
Who's there?
William.
William who?
William mind your own business?

Being attracted to someone of the same sex is not a new phenomenon. LGBT people have been around since the dawn of time, and we have been parents since the dawn of time as well. We may not have always been open about our sexuality while we were parents, but that doesn't mean we didn't exist. It used to be common for LGBT people to marry someone of the opposite sex and have children in an attempt to hide who they really were because they feared societal repercussions. LGBT people feared being disowned by their families, fired from their jobs, jailed, beaten, or even killed. While some of these fears still exist in our country, we've come a long way and have had numerous advances in LGBT equality over the last few decades. More and more people have come out of the closet and are proud of who they are. We can thank Stonewall, Pride marches, Harvey Milk, Obama, and numerous LGBT activists for that.

But just because we have more rights and are generally living more open lives, doesn't mean that everything is lah-di-dah. While same-sex parenting isn't a new phenomenon, "visible" same-sex parenting is. Television shows like Modern Family and The Fosters may have introduced people to the concept and reality of same-sex parents, but many people still haven't encountered LGBT families in person. We're like unicorns to some people: they've heard about gay parents but haven't really seen any. Because of this, you're probably going to be asked a lot of personal and invasive questions. Some people are genuinely curious and are trying to learn more about how adoption, surrogacy, and same-sex parenting works. Other people already have their heads full of negative assumptions.

It's OK to have mixed emotions when you get these kinds of questions, and your answers to them may change depending on your mood at the time or how much sleep you've had the night before. The challenge is finding a way to provide educational information while also protecting your child's privacy. Keep in mind that as your child gets older, they will be observing and listening to how you answer these prying questions, so you'll want to answer in a way that doesn't give them the assumption that something is wrong with their family unit. That being said, you don't owe anyone answers to questions about your personal life either. It's up to you whether or not you want to engage. Here are a few common questions you may get along with suggestions for ways you can respond.

Where Is His/Her Mother?

It's very common for strangers to ask this question, especially if a dad is out alone with an infant, and it could be asked for a variety of reasons. Maybe the person is just trying to make small talk with you. Maybe they think you have kidnapped the child, or maybe they feel bad for you, a male (who can't possibly know how to parent) being left to fend for himself while the mom (who obviously is the only one who can take care of a child) is somewhere else. Keep in mind that most of the time the person asking the question is not trying to be mean or negative. They might be assuming that there is a mother somewhere in the picture, or who knows, they may be curious about adoption, foster care, or surrogacy and are thinking you might be able to help them by answering a few questions.

Here are some possibilities for how you might answer this question. Remember, your child may be listening, so your answers might change as they get older. Also, it's best to keep your answers short with strangers unless you want to open things up for the person to ask additional questions about your personal situation. Try one of these answers.

- "My husband and I are the parents."
- "Why do you ask?"
- "There is no mom. He/she has two dads."

Which One of You Is the Dad?

If you and your partner are both out with your child, strangers may ask this question, assuming a mom is in the picture somewhere and dad is just hanging out with a friend. The quick and easy answer to this one is, "We both are."

REAL-LIFE STORY:

"Before our daughter could talk, we would often get, 'She is so precious, which one of you is her daddy?' We would then begin this eloquent and awkward dialogue of saying, 'We both are,' multiple times until we finally got the tilted head stare. We refer to this as the 'dog-whistle look.' You whistle, and a dog will tilt its head."

–Trey Darnell

Which One of You Is the "Real" Dad?

This is an attempt to find out whose sperm was used, with the assumption being that the one who is biologically related is the "real" parent. The person may even flat-out ask which one of you donated your sperm. If you're not comfortable talking about it, try one of these answers:

- "Does it matter?"

- "Why do you ask?"

- "We both are his/her 'real' parents."

REAL-LIFE STORY:

"The awkward question that we get most frequently is about the genetic relationship we have with our children. Again, we understand it is a natural curiosity, so we try not to be offended by the question. We have two sets of twins and both are mixed-race Asian and Caucasian, so it becomes a bit of a guessing game trying to figure out which half of the interracial gay couple is biologically related to each of these kids. Once, when our older children were still babies, we went out to lunch and the waitress asked us almost immediately after introducing herself, 'Who is the sperm donor?' We were so shocked with her forward approach that I frankly don't recall if we responded with an order for the avocado egg rolls appetizer or our standard response. We usually tell people that we keep that detail private because we want to be treated equally as parents to all our kids. The waitress' gay coworker overheard the exchange and was so mortified. He came to our rescue and took over our table for her." –David Hu

Which One of You Is the Mom?

This question assumes one parent is feminine and the other is masculine, or one of you does what they consider "feminine roles" and the other does what they consider "masculine roles." It's similar to when someone asks an engaged same-sex couple, "Which one of you is the bride?" You can joke around and say one of you is the mom if you'd like. Or you can say, "Neither. We're both dads."

What Is It like to Be a Gay Dad?

Well, the first thing we do in the morning is wake our kids up by playing loud dance music. Then we feed them protein shakes for breakfast, and spend time together gossiping while doing each other's hair. When it's time for school, we ride our magical unicorns there while waving rainbow flags, and when school is over, we hit the gym and work out for a bit before making our way to the club. No, gay dads are not different from straight parents. We feed our kids, clothe them, take them to school, read them bedtime stories, and everything else parents do. The simple answer to this is that we're just like other parents.

Who Does All the Mommy Stuff?

This question is horrible because it implies that it's a woman's job to do certain things like cooking, cleaning, feeding babies, and changing diapers. There are a few different ways you can answer this question:

- "We equally share parenting responsibilities."
- "What do you mean, mommy stuff?"
- "We don't believe jobs should be based on gender."

Why Did She Give Him/Her Up? I Could Never Give Up My Child.

Statements and questions like these stem from people having no real-life experience with how open adoption works. It used to be the case that the majority of adoptions in the United States were closed, and children grew up without knowing who their birthparents were. There was no contact between the birthparents and the adopted children, hence the thought process that mothers had "given" their children away and wanted nothing to do with them anymore. For many birthmothers, that couldn't be further from the truth. Many of them continued to think about their children, wondering if they were OK and whether they had made the right choice or not.

In today's day and age, the majority of infant adoptions in the United States are done through open adoption, allowing the birthparents and adopted children to have contact with each other after the adoption. Today, most birthmothers don't "give their children up" for adoption; they spend time trying to find the perfect family to place their children with when they know they are not in a position to parent themselves. Adoption doesn't mean the birthmother doesn't want the child, it means that she thought long and hard to make the best decision for her child. It takes a lot of thought, courage, and emotional strength to make a decision like that. Here are a few responses you might want to try out:

- "She didn't give him/her up. She made a difficult decision to do what was in the best interest of her child, and to give him/her a life that she could not provide."

- "She didn't give him/her up. She's still part of his/her life."

- "That's not my story to tell."

What If Your Child Turns Out to Be Gay?

As if something is wrong with someone being gay. If they are assuming a parent's sexual orientation determines a child's orientation, that's a false assumption. Here are a few suggestions for how you can respond:

- "I'd still love them, just like I would if they turn out to be straight."

- "Why? Do you think being gay is a bad thing?"

- "My parents were straight and that didn't make me straight."

What If Your Child Is Straight?

Maybe the person asking this question is assuming you won't be able to identify with your child if he or she turns out to be straight. A great way to respond to this question is to just repeat it back to them: "What if my child is straight?"

How Did You Get Him/Her/Them?

The person asking most likely wants to know how you formed your family. Did you pursue adoption, foster care, or surrogacy? Maybe they're being nosy or, again, maybe they are genuinely interested in learning how those avenues work. The way you should answer this depends on how open you want to be with the person. Do you want to explain the whole journey to parenthood with them, or do you want to change the topic? Again, remember: you don't owe an answer to anyone, so don't feel bad for not giving them the whole background.

> *REAL-LIFE STORY:*
> *"People ask about how we created our family all the time. I try to remember that mostly people are curious, and the vast majority of the time this comes from a place of support. Still, it can feel quite invasive, especially in the wrong contexts. I try to answer completely because I think one of the important ways we gain equality is by educating people about our families. But I am also careful not to share too much—knowing that we are a family through adoption is usually enough."* **–Gabriel Blau**

REAL-LIFE STORY:

"The question we get that sometimes irritates us is, 'How did you get them?'...like we went to a shopping market and picked them out from a display case. We recognize that these questions are often asked out of curiosity and not malice. We use this as an opportunity to educate people about how our family was formed and that we are not unique in our desire to be parents. If people are genuine about their questions, we will get as detailed as they want. We have even gone as far as to explain about our choices for egg donors and a surrogate if they really want to know. Sometimes they have just never had an opportunity to meet people with experiences like ours." –Tommy Starling

REAL-LIFE STORY:

"The most common question is, 'How did we get her?' While she was born here in the US, she looks Asian, and conversations start with something along those lines. Because of this, we get compared to the gay dads on Modern Family a lot. We were travelling to NYC, and the guy sitting in the seat next to me called his wife to tell her that he was sitting next to a real-life Cam and Mitchell. As I said it happens regularly–at first it was fun, but now it's just old." –Chad Scanlon

Where Did You Get Him/Her/Them?

This question is common when people adopt or foster children of a different race. Many times, there is an assumption that the parents adopted the child from a different country. The way you answer this, again, depends on how much you want to engage with the person. You could call them on it and ask, "Why do you want to know?" You could go ahead and tell them the details of your journey to parenthood, or you could even give a sarcastic answer. "At the bakery. I heard that's where they keep the buns in the oven." Keep in mind though, sarcastic answers may just lead to additional questions and your child might be listening to your answer too.

REAL-LIFE STORY:
"Because our children are adopted and are a different race, the most common question we get is, 'Where are they from?' While we do like to educate others and want to represent families that may look different well, we evade the question when it's asked in front of them. They are from here. Because they are black, there is this automatic assumption that we adopted from Africa. Sometimes I want to say, 'You do know that there are black people from the United States.' Of course we don't, but it would be nice if people used the filter, 'Would you want a stranger asking questions about your children in front of them?'" –Duke Nelson

---

How Much Did He/She/They Cost?

This could be another example of someone being genuinely curious about the practicalities of adoption, foster care, or surrogacy. They may be interested in starting their own family the same way, but not sure if they can afford the fees associated with it. Still, the question is as appropriate as asking another person how much their salary is. Your answer could be honest, blunt, sincere, or sarcastic. It's up to you.

- "He/she/they didn't cost anything."
- "Eighteen years of our lives."

REAL-LIFE STORY:
"The most awkward question (in the beginning at least) was, 'How much did she cost?' At first we just laughed uncomfortably and changed the subject, but two years in we tend to say, 'As much as a Prius.' That turns the table on who's uncomfortable. Who really asks how much a human being costs?" –Chad Scanlon

How Did You Get Stuck with the Kids? Is It Mom's Day Out? Are You Babysitting?

These questions assume dads are only taking care of the children because the mother is not available at the time. We have an opportunity here to change society's way of thinking. Taking care of children is not a "mom's" job; it's a "parent's" job. Try one of these responses:

- "I'm not 'stuck' with the kids. I cherish every minute I have with them."
- "Not every family has a mom."
- "Our child is lucky to have two dads."
- "Parenting is not a woman's job. It's a parent's job."
- "Fathers don't 'babysit.'"

> ### REAL-LIFE STORY:
> "I remember meeting a friend of mine for dinner and having my son in a stroller. As we were leaving, the hostess came up to me and patted me on the back saying, 'You are such a good babysitter!' That one comment has stuck with me for years. It felt like someone saying, 'You obviously couldn't be this child's parent.' We also had a lot of people come up so they could give us their unsolicited approval. 'You guys are so great,' or, 'It's so great that you're doing this!' I was never doing anything outside of what other parents would do, and I definitely wasn't doing anything great at the time. I would just be like picking my kids up from school or something like that." –Rob Watson

> ### REAL-LIFE STORY:
> "When we go grocery shopping or out to dinner, we often get the, 'Oh, you must be giving mom a day off' comment. We are quick to respond that there is no mom and that our kids are lucky and happy to have two dads. We never want our children to think there is anything wrong with their family or that they need to hide something." –Tommy Starling

How Old Was He/She When You Got Him/Her?

This question is quite common, and comes with an assumption that since you're a gay dad, you probably adopted or went through foster care. It's up to you if you want to go into details about your family expansion journey.

REAL-LIFE STORY:

"This type of question is usually presented to us as: 'How long have you had him?' or, 'How old was he when you adopted him?' Because our son was conceived via surrogacy and subsequently adopted, we typically say something like: 'We adopted him soon after he was born,' or 'He's been ours since he was born.' We provide basic information without going into detail." **–Michael Hadley**

REAL-LIFE STORY:

"Most people are capable of realizing that we are gay parents, but curiosity often leads them to question how our family came to be. People often assume our kids were adopted, and we have been asked, 'How old where they when you got them?' several times over the years. We understand that most people don't know about surrogacy, so we take no offense to these questions. We explain that our kids were born through surrogacy. This frequently starts a discussion about the complexities of gestational surrogacy. We would like to think we have opened some minds and educated some people in these conversations." **–David Hu**

> **REAL-LIFE STORY:**
> "We often get asked, 'How old was he when you got him?' Luckily we don't get offended very easily, and our lives are pretty much an open book, so we don't mind answering these questions. We explain our surrogacy journey and hopefully next time people will think twice about asking invasive questions." –BJ Barone

Aren't You Worried Your Child Will Be Bullied for Having Same-Sex Parents?

Look, everyone gets made fun of at some point. It's a fact of life. You are either too tall or too small, too skinny or overweight. Your hair is too frizzy, your teeth are too crooked, or your face is too pimply. Someone is always going to find something to tease you about.

The important thing is that we teach our children to be confident and proud of who they are. We can teach them to stand up for themselves, and we can foster an environment where our children are comfortable coming to us (or another trusted adult) whenever there's a problem. We can also lead by example.

What About Your Child's "Real" Parents?

The person asking most likely wants to know about the birthparents or the donors, but doesn't know how to phrase the question. First of all, you can answer the question if you are comfortable doing so, but it's none of their business and you don't have to answer if you don't want to. Second of all, you are the "real" parents!

Do You Think You Might Be Depriving Your Child of a Female Role Model?

Where do people come up with these ideas? It's not like we're raising our children on an island inhabited by men only. There are plenty of women in our lives that can be role models: grandmothers, sisters, aunts, nieces, teachers, friends, and neighbors. Take a pick.

How to Find LGBT-Friendly Schools

The school years can offer wonderful experiences for kids, but they can also be stressful too. It's important to find a school that will be welcoming to your child and your family, but how do you know if the school you're looking into is LGBT-friendly? Most schools will tell you that they're accepting and that they don't discriminate against anyone, but how do you make sure they are walking the walk and not just talking the talk?

It's important to keep in mind that all schools will tell you how great they are. Don't just talk to them on the phone and take their word for it. Visit the school yourself and check things out in person. Ask for referrals.

Below is a list of things to consider when researching new schools for your child. Don't feel obligated to get answers to everything on the list. Rather, use it as a guide and ask the questions that allow you to get a good feel for the school's acceptance of the LGBT community. Keep in mind that some of these points (like gender-neutral forms) are relevant to all schools, regardless of grade level. Other suggestions may be more relevant for secondary schools than for elementary schools or preschools.

REAL-LIFE STORY:

"When I was trying to enroll my kids in school, I noticed that several of the private schools had no issues with same-sex parents, but they did seem to have issues with kids that had learning challenges. They wanted to gloat about how smart their kids were and basically tried to screen out kids with challenges. My kids were from the foster care system and were exposed to drugs in utero, so they did have learning challenges. I remember one school wouldn't even talk to us. They wrote a letter to us saying we should do homeschooling. We tried looking into non-private schools too, but it was a challenge finding ones that weren't religious. The counselor at one of the Christian schools said our kids would be welcomed there, but he would tell them the same thing he tells kids with divorced parents: 'Your family is not God's plan for a family.' Yay, that seemed welcoming." –Rob Watson

What Is the Diversity Like in the School?

Understanding the school's diversity dynamics could give you a better idea for how sympathetic the staff is to the needs of students with various backgrounds. Are there other kids in the school with LGBT parents? Also look for other types of diversity that are not necessarily LGBT related: for example, race, religion, economic backgrounds, disabilities, etc.

Olivia Higgins, founder of Queerly Elementary, says that we can even go a step further. "Expand your evaluation of a school's diversity beyond just the demographics of the students and families. A faculty that reflects a broad spectrum of identities suggests the school may be a more welcoming place for everyone."

What Does the School's Website Look Like?

Sometimes you can get a good feel about a school from their website, so look over the information they provide online. What do their mission statement, vision, and school policies say? What type of school activities do they promote? Are staff pictures and bios posted? If so, remember to look for diversity within the staff.

What Do the Forms Look Like?

If you want your child to attend a specific school, you'll be required to complete their enrollment forms. Before filling anything out, look to see what type of language is used. Do they have words like "mother" and "father," or do they use more gender-neutral language like "parent" or "guardian"? The latter words are more inclusive and not just for kids with LGBT parents. They can refer to children who are raised by single parents or grandparents, too.

It's possible that a school can be accepting of diversity but may not have thought about changing their forms. If that's the case, you can help explain that by using more inclusive terminology, the school will be sending a more positive and welcoming message to students and their families.

Posters and Signage

When doing a physical tour of the school, be on the lookout for inclusive signage throughout the campus. Look for signs that show acceptance of all families or posters that say something like, "Everyone belongs here." Do the signs encourage people to be themselves and are they welcoming to everyone? Did you see a rainbow anywhere? You can also look out for GSA signs or "Safe Space" signs.

What Types of Books Are Used in the School?

Because books are used as teaching tools, you can get a good idea for the school's values by observing the types of books available in their library. Don't just ask if they have diverse books. Ask to see their library and then ask to see a few examples. Are their books diverse? Do they have any with LGBT families or diverse family structures? Do they have options where the main characters are different genders and races, or are they all the same? If religious books are present, do they favor one religion or are others represented as well?

Higgins says not to worry too much if you see a lack of these types of books in the beginning. "If your child's classroom or school library lacks books that reflect a wide range of perspectives, you can work with the librarian or classroom teacher to suggest new books to purchase. The Parent-Teacher Association (PTA) may be willing to help develop a book list and perhaps even raise funds for those new books."

For older grades, there's often a book list detailing what will be read during the year for each of the different grade levels. Don't be afraid to ask for a copy of the list so you can review it and see how diverse the reading is. You may even want to make suggestions for books that can be added. Regardless of grade level, being exposed to diversity in books can help students learn about acceptance while also giving them a greater chance to see themselves in the stories they read.

How Does the School Embrace or Honor Different Types of Families?

Families are discussed throughout our school journeys, from preschool to high school. Whether kids are drawing pictures of their families, mapping out their family trees, or taking courses on genetics, family structures are going to be brought up. Ask what types of projects the classes do on families and how they address various types of family structures. Are family pictures hung on the classroom wall, and if so, how will teachers address questions about your family from other kids or parents?

What Is the School's Anti-Discrimination Policy?

Reading a school's anti-discrimination policy is a good way to get an idea for how they feel about the LGBT community. Check to see if they prohibit discrimination on the basis of sexual orientation and gender identity. It's even better if they have language that prohibits discrimination based on the "actual or perceived" sexual orientation or gender identity of the student or because of anyone whom the student associates with. That means no one is allowed to discriminate against a student because he or she has LGBT friends or family members.

How Does the School Handle Bullying?

All schools pretty much have policies against bullying. Ask them how they define bullying, what they have in place to prevent it, and what actions they take when bullying occurs. Do they have classroom rules, and if so, what are they? Schools that take bullying seriously go out of their way to establish a safe school environment. To learn more about bullying at schools, go to www.stopbullying.gov.

REAL-LIFE STORY:

"It is important to us, living in Northeast Tennessee, that we are active in our daughter's life and her preschool. We are very open and forward with the school director and the preschool staff. Prior to enrolling our daughter in preschool, we visited the school, and we did not hide being a gay couple. Direct questions were asked regarding acceptance, behavior, and bullying. We do not just use the carpool line to drop off our daughter for school. One of us will always park and walk her in to her classroom. This allows us to become familiar with the staff and students.

"One day, my husband Matthew dropped off Harper for early care. Harper interacted with children of all ages during this hour before school actually started.

Harper's classmates know me as her Daddy, but were not familiar with Matthew. Harper began to cry when her classmates were telling her that Matthew was not her daddy. The teacher had everyone sit down and immediately began to teach the kids about how every family is different and Harper just happened to have two dads. Because we were present and active within the school, the teacher was able to take this opportunity and turn it into a learning experience for everyone. "While we see every family as different and find it fascinating, we do have to 'stay ahead of the game' and educate teachers and the school. At Harper's age, we are lucky that kids are still impressionable. We try to be positive male and fatherly role models and allow Harper's teachers and classmates to see that while we may be considered different, we are not that different. Harper's teachers are very good at recognizing who did Harper's hair that day. Is there a class for dads on how to do their daughters' hair?"
–Trey Darnell

What Does the School Do to Minimize Gender Segregation?

Sometimes schools can place limits and restrictions on people based on gender without even knowing it. For example, they may have boys line up in one line and girls line up in another. Other times it's more obvious, like requiring gender-specific dress codes. Is the school you're researching conscious of these practices, and if so, what do they do to minimize gender segregation? Here are some things you can ask about gender practices.

- **Activities** – Are students allowed to participate in sports teams and extracurricular activities in accordance with their gender identity?

- **Dress Codes** – Are gender-based uniforms required at the school, and if so, are students allowed to wear uniforms in accordance with their gender identity? Are students allowed to express themselves by wearing gender-neutral or gender non-conforming clothing?

- **Facilities** – Does the school allow students to use bathrooms and lockers rooms based on their gender identity, or do they require students to use facilities according to their sex assigned at birth?

These policies will not only give you insight into how the school treats transgender students, but it will show you how accepting they are to people's differences and if they foster a safe environment that helps students become confident and comfortable as individuals.

Does the School Honor LGBT Awareness and/or LGBT-Inclusive Events?

October is LGBT History Month, and it offers schools the opportunity to teach students about diversity and the important roles LGBT people have played in society. It can be celebrated in all grade levels, from talking about diverse family structures in earlier grades, to learning about significant role models like Alan Turing, Bayard Rustin, Renée Richards, Sally Ride, and Harvey Milk in higher grade levels. Research by GLSEN (originally called the Gay, Lesbian, & Straight Education Network) has found that LGBT-inclusive curricula contribute to safer school environments and increased peer acceptance. Here are a few other LGBT awareness events that can be honored or recognized in schools.

- **March 31** – International Transgender Day of Visibility
- **April** (day varies year-to-year) – Day of Silence
- **First Sunday of May** – International Family Equality Day
- **May 17** – International Day Against Homophobia and Transphobia (IDAHO or IDAHOT)
- **May 22** – Harvey Milk Day
- **June** – Pride Month
- **September 23** – International Celebrate Bisexuality Day or Bi Visibility Day
- **October** – LGBT History Month (USA)
- **October 11** – National Coming Out Day
- **Third Thursday in October** – Spirit Day
- **November 20** – Transgender Day of Remembrance
- **December 1** – World AIDS Day
- **December 10** – Human Rights Day

Does the School Have a Gay Straight Alliance (GSA) or LGBT Club?

GSAs are open to all students regardless of sexual orientation or gender identity, and their presence on campus may have a positive impact on a school's climate. They may also provide evidence of a school's commitment to LGBT students and their allies.

Does the School Provide Comprehensive Sex Education?

If sex education is taught at the school, check to see whether they provide information that is inclusive of LGBT youth, and make sure that the content covered is medically and scientifically accurate. If you want to take it a step further, you can even ask about the review process the curriculum goes through. Are there ongoing community groups that review the content? If so, who's involved? Parents? Teachers? Employees? Some schools may even have a parent night where they allow parents to ask questions about the curriculum. They can see what videos are being watched and what books are being read. If you want to verify the content, take the opportunity to do so.

What Are the Rules Pertaining to Student Relationships?

Are same-sex couples allowed to date and display affection at school on the same terms as opposite-sex student couples? If the school has dances, are students allowed to attend with someone of the same gender?

Do the Teachers and/or Faculty Go Through Any Type of Training on LGBT Issues?

There are all kinds of professional development courses to help teachers and faculty foster a welcoming school environment. Here are some of the things training can cover:

- Understanding different types of family structures
- Learning how to reduce gender stereotyping
- Using inclusive language
- Understanding the needs of LGBT students
- Learning how to answer questions relating to LGBT topics
- Recognizing and preventing bullying
- Providing safe spaces

If your school would like more information on training for teachers and faculty, the following websites are great resources:

Queerly Elementary
www.queerlyelementary.com

GLSEN
www.glsen.org

HRC's Welcoming Schools Program
www.welcomingschools.org

Southern Poverty Law Center's Teaching Tolerance Program
www.tolerance.org

There's a lot to consider when researching schools, and it's easy to get overwhelmed. Before you make the final decision, take a moment to breathe and reflect on the various things the school has to offer. "Same-sex families may be tempted to simply focus on picking a school based on how LGBTQ-friendly it seems to be," says Higgins. "However, don't lose sight of the many other equally important factors to help you decide on the best school for your child such as: location, before/after school care, cost, art and music programs, specific academic and social needs of your child, teacher-student ratio, curriculum, homework policy, adequate recess, physical education program, etc."

What to Do on
Mother's Day

Some people have a mom and a dad. Some people have two moms or two dads. Some people only have one parent, while others may have multiple stepparents. Some children are raised by extended family members, like aunts, uncles, or grandparents, and some people don't have parents at all. All families are different. I know this, you know this, but other people don't necessarily know this.

Take Mother's Day and Father's Day for example. Lots of people, especially educators in schools, often assume that children have a mother and a father. They don't always take into consideration that some kids live in single-parent households, have LGBT parents, or maybe no parents at all. It may get awkward if your child has to make and bring home a Mother's Day gift. Will your child get confused? Will they get teased for not having a mom? Will they make the gift anyway and decide which dad to give it to?

One of the best things you can do is to take this opportunity to discuss family diversity with your child. Have a conversation about how all families are different and why their family is special. Remind them how much they are loved. In addition, explain your family situation to your child's school and ask them whether the classes celebrate Mother's Day. If they do, have a conversation about how you celebrate it in your home. It's important to keep in mind that not all families with gay dads celebrate Mother's Day in the same way, so even if the school has had children with gay dads in the past, this doesn't necessarily mean that they know how your family celebrates the holiday.

For example, look at all the different ways LGBT families are created. Some of our children were adopted and may or may not know their birthparents. Some of our children were born via surrogacy and may or may not know their egg donors or surrogates. Some of our children were in foster care and may or may not know their birth families. So on Mother's Day, do we celebrate birth families, surrogates, egg donors, or a combination thereof—or do we say our children don't have mothers? The answer honestly is, you do whatever you think is best for you, your family, and your child.

I talked to a bunch of other gay dads about Mother's Day. Here's what I asked them and what they told me.

How does Mother's Day work for your family? Do you celebrate the holiday? If so, how? If you don't celebrate it, what happens when your kids are in school and the class does a Mother's Day project?

"Mother's Day has evolved in our family. Our kids didn't know their birthmother when they were younger, so we wrote on balloons, said a prayer, and released them into the air to honor her. My son met his birthmother when he got older, but it wasn't a good experience, so we don't do that anymore. Now we spend the holiday with their grandmother."
—Jay Foxworthy

"Our family celebrates my husband on Mother's Day and me on Father's Day. As gay parents, we decided that we needed to take Mother's Day to celebrate one of us! Why not? The kids and I typically make something (hand/finger prints, art projects, cards, etc.) for my husband, and we cook or go out to dinner. Pretty typical of what straight couples with children would do for their mother on the day. We call it 'Daddies Day.'"
—Adam White

"We celebrate Mother's Day by honoring the women in our lives. At our son's daycare, they make Mother's Day cards and gifts, and we give them to our mothers (our son's grandmas). We buy gifts for our moms and take them out for Mother's Day brunch."
—BJ Barone

"Our daughter is still young enough not to realize Mother's Day is anything other than another day. As far as celebrating the day, we spend it with my husband's aunt, who is like a mother to us: she lives in the area and she is known as Nana. For our first Mother's Day we FaceTimed with our daughter's mother, but this past year she was on drugs and we skipped that for all of our benefits. Other family members acknowledge the day to celebrate both of us."
—Chad Scanlon

"My kids are not the only kids at their school without mothers. Some of their classmates take the opportunity to honor and celebrate their grandmothers, social workers, or other special women in their lives. For us, Mother's Day is Fommy (Father–Mommy) Day since my sons don't have a mom. As far as schools go, I think it's important that we, as gay dads, get involved and make an effort to get to know your child's teachers. That way, there are fewer chances of surprises."
—David Aguirre

"We have not found Mother's Day to be a major problem. Most teachers have asked us how we would like to handle Mother's Day projects, and we gladly let them know something can be made for their grandmothers, one of whom lives very nearby. This past Mother's Day, my husband's mother was able to be the guest of honor at the preschool Mother's Day show, where she was given

a decorated apron and treated to a song and dance performed by two of her grandchildren. She loved it! We are raising our children Jewish, so we have grown very accustomed to holidays being celebrated at school that are either not celebrated at all or occur without as much fanfare at our home. On the other hand, Father's Day and all the kids' birthdays fall after the end of the school year in Florida. So just like the Jewish holidays, we make sure to celebrate Father's Day and their birthdays at home or on vacation over the summer months, to make sure the kids don't feel like they are missing out."
—David Hu

"When my son was younger, the teachers would make it more inclusive and it would be celebrated as 'Parent's Day' rather than Mother's Day. If a project was made, he would make it for one of his grandmas instead."
—Del Hubers

"We adopted our son internationally, and he was in an orphanage from his first day. We don't know anything about his birthmother, but through comments, we acknowledge her and her gift/journey every year on Mother's Day. Our daughter was born via gestational surrogacy. We have an ongoing relationship with our daughter's surrogate and celebrate her directly on Mother's Day. Additionally, we celebrate the many mothers in our lives: aunts, grandmothers, godmothers, etc."
—Elliott Kronenfeld

"We celebrate by FaceTiming our mothers and avoiding brunch locations. Seriously, I hate long waits, even more so with kids. We literally got a family membership at the local zoo on Mother's Day in order to skip the line. I had not anticipated that the zoo was a Mother's Day destination. Our kids are in preschool and first grade. So far, the kids'

schools have been pretty respectful. We have received very nice non-gendered gifts from our kids that the other kids made for their moms."
—Ian Hart

"We celebrate Mother's Day by honoring aunts, grandmas, and other important women in our lives. We still have contact with our daughter's surrogate and we celebrate her for Mother's Day too since we couldn't have become parents without her. Our daughter is two now, and she has met our surrogate, but she doesn't currently do anything for her on Mother's Day. We think it's important to wait until she's older and can decide for herself if that's something she wants to do."
—Shawn Moore

"We celebrate Mother's Day over brunch with my husband's parents. Our son had a couple of Mother's Day projects when he was in preschool and kindergarten. He gave both of them to my mother-in-law."
—Michael Hadley

"We generally celebrate Mother's Day by celebrating with other members of our family who are Mothers. Typically, we would give Mother's Day cards to their Grandmother. In school the kids would make a project for Grandma and for Papa and Daddy."
—Mike Degala

"Mother's Day, for us, is a day to celebrate our children's grandmother. The school is very supportive and inclusive and allows my mom to attend their Mother's Day activities. Our children make cards for their grandmother and give her any crafts they may make at school."
—Tommy Starling

Mother's Day and Father's Day are based on good intentions to honor the roles that parents play in our lives, but in this day and age, do we really need to separate parents by gender? Especially when we look at same-sex parents. More often than not, we share parental responsibilities. If you're looking to be creative with how you celebrate your family, consider celebrating one of the following holidays:

- **Parent's Day** – 4th Sunday in July
- **Son and Daughter Day** – August 11
- **National Stepfamily Day** – September 16
- **Working Parents Day** – September 16
- **National Adoption Awareness Month** – November (whole month)
- **National Adoption Day** – Saturday before Thanksgiving
- **Universal Children's Day** – November 20
- **International Children's Day** – 2nd Sunday in December

Childproofing
Round Two – Older
Children

Childproofing isn't just something you do for infants and toddlers. It's something you're going to need to revisit every once in a while as your child gets older and becomes more independent, especially with technology. Here are a few suggestions to consider when childproofing your home for older children. Because each family is different, you will need to determine which rules, guidelines, and controls you are comfortable with implementing.

Television

There is a lot of content available on TV that may not be appropriate for your children to watch. Most television shows have TV Parental Guidelines to give parents more information about the age-appropriateness of each program; however, news and sports programs are exempt from these ratings. A device called the V-Chip has been built into most modern television sets and allows parents to block programs based on the TV Parental Guidelines.

Check with your cable company to see what controls they offer and how to implement them. You should be able to block individual programs based on ratings and channels. You can even block adult titles from showing up in the electronic program guide. Here are the different types of ratings used for television.

AUDIENCE LABELS:

TV-Y (All Children): Appropriate for all children, and the themes are specifically designed for a very young audience.

TV-Y7 (Directed to Older Children): Appropriate for children age seven and older.

TV-G (General Audience): Suitable for children and adults. The program may not be designed specifically for children; however, it contains little or no violence, no strong language, and no sexual dialogue or situations.

TV-PG (Parental Guidance Suggested): May contain material unsuitable for younger children, such as suggestive dialogue, coarse language, sexual situations, or moderate violence.

TV-14 (Parents Strongly Cautioned): The program may contain more intense suggestive dialogue, coarse language, sexual situations, or moderate violence.

TV-MA (Mature Audience Only): Unsuitable for children under seventeen and may contain offensive language, explicit sexual activity, and/or graphic violence.

TIP:
Some televisions have the ability to connect to the Internet and install apps. In addition to setting parental controls on your TV, you may need to set them up for your apps too. For example, you may want to consider enabling Netflix's parental controls to prevent your kids from watching inappropriate content through the app on your TV.

Computers, Laptops, and the Internet

Anything and everything is available on the Internet these days, so you'll want to make sure you proof the devices in your home accordingly if your child will have access to them. Each operating system and Internet browser will have different ways to set parental controls, and since technology changes frequently, I won't go into details on how to set them in order to prevent the information here from becoming outdated quickly. Rather, I will give you an idea for what you should be aware of. You can search online for how to set the controls on your specific device, and you can set the controls for what you feel is appropriate for your children.

The good thing is that you can set up different controls for different users. This means you can access the same device as your child, but you can give yourself freer rein than you allow your kids.

Time Limits – You can set time limits on your computer and/or devices. You can allow a certain amount of time (for example, an hour or two a day) or you can prevent access during certain times. This is helpful for when you want a device to shut off when it's bedtime.

Email and Messaging – Some mail and instant messaging applications may allow you to set restrictions so that emails can only be sent to certain contacts.

Dictionary – You may want to check your computer to see if you can limit inappropriate content (such as profanity) from appearing in dictionaries and thesauruses.

Camera – You may or may not want to prevent access to the camera so that your children are not making themselves visible to strangers online.

Websites – You can set the controls to allow only specific sites geared towards children, or you can choose to block certain sites.

Web Browsers – There are various types of browsers that can be used to surf the Net: Internet Explorer, Safari, Firefox, Chrome, etc. Each of them runs independently of the others, so if you have more than one on your system, you will need to set up parental controls on each of them.

Internet History – If you share a computer, depending on what sites you visit, you may want to delete your own browser history.

YouTube – A Restricted Mode is available on YouTube to filter out mature content. This works on a browser level, so you will have to turn it on for each browser you use.

Online Games – Depending on your operating system, you may be able to restrict what games can be played or accessed.

REAL-LIFE STORY:

"I had to block a few video games because of inappropriate things, like excessive violence or cussing. If I saw them playing things they shouldn't be playing, I would talk to them about it and shut it down. It's sort of a losing battle in a way, but I think it's important to have these types of conversations with them. Many online games connect to the Internet and allow people to interact with other gamers. They talk about their characters and all kinds of things about their lives. When my son went online to play, he would be open about everything and would tell people he had gay dads. Eventually, he started getting harassed by other players online because of this, and they would call my son gay too: actually, not in a negative way. 'Dude, it's nothing to be ashamed of...' He got frustrated because it was not who he is. We had a conversation about blocking people who did not respect his identity." –Rob Watson

Gaming Consoles – There are lots of restrictions you can put in place such as restricting certain games based on ratings, restricting DVDs based on ratings, and preventing online usage and web browsing.

Social Media – Social media sites like Facebook, Twitter, and Instagram have become a major part of our lives, and eventually, your kids are going to want to be on those sites too. Consider taking a few precautions to keep your children safe from online predators:

- You can adjust the privacy settings on your child's social media accounts to make it harder for strangers to find them and prevent them from seeing posts.

- Some parents establish rules with their children allowing them to access their child's social media account upon request.

TIP:

Before your child uses the Internet, it's a good idea to talk to them and set a few expectations. Let them know what is acceptable for online usage and what sites to stay away from. Consider keeping the computer in a visible location, like a living room, so you can supervise online activity. Make sure your kids know they should never give out personal information online, such as names, addresses, email addresses, passwords, where they go to school, etc., and let them know that if someone bullies them online or makes them uncomfortable, they should talk to you, a teacher, or another grown-up they can trust.

Wireless Phones and Tablets

At some point in time, your kid is bound to get ahold of your cell phone. Maybe you decide to let them play a game, or they pick it up after you've set it down. Either way, you may want to consider having a password on your phone so they can't access it on their own. Other things you may want to consider:

- Make sure you don't have any compromising pictures on your phone that they could see by scrolling through your photos. (Don't worry, I won't judge.)

- Think about the types of apps you have on your phone and ask yourself if there's anything you wouldn't want them to see.

Many parents make the decision to give children their own phones or tablets when they get a bit older. Maybe you want to be able to call them when they are out with their friends, or maybe you want them to have the ability to call you in case of an emergency. Whatever the reason may be, if you give your child a device that can connect to the Internet, here are a few protections you may want to put in place:

Purchase Blocker – Unless you want your bill to skyrocket, it might be a good idea to put blockers in place to prohibit your kids from making purchases that are directly billed to you. This includes apps, games with in-app purchases, ringtones, and more.

Usage Restrictions – You can set limits on things like texts and data usage to keep your costs down. You can also apply other restrictions, such as who can be called and what content can be accessed online. Check with your wireless provider to see what kind of parental controls they have so you can make the best decision for your family.

Geotracking – This is the ability to identify a person's location by using the GPS data from their phone or other GPS-enabled device. You can do things like make sure your child arrives home safely from school, or set up alerts if they travel outside predetermined boundaries. If this is something you're interested in, your wireless provider can help you enable it.

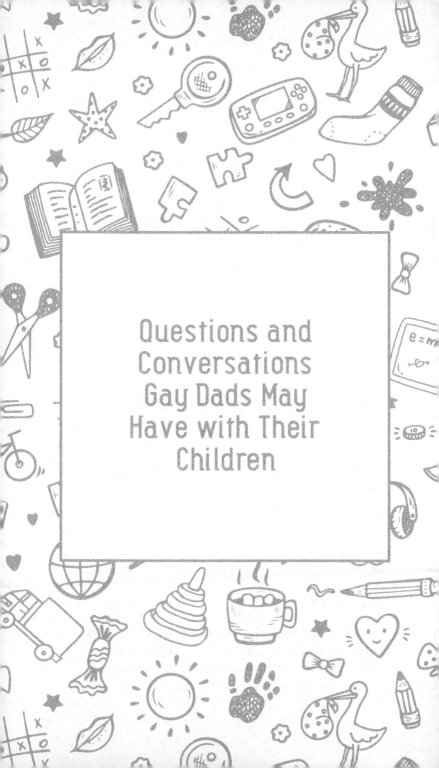

Questions and Conversations Gay Dads May Have with Their Children

As a gay dad, there are lots of conversations you might have with your children that straight parents wouldn't typically have with their kids. For example, explaining how our families are different, conversations about LGBT bullying, explaining why people want laws passed that negatively impact our families, etc. Some of the topics are unique to our families, while others are common conversations that may be discussed differently in LGBT households. For example, some parents might have the "birds and the bees" talk solely to explain where babies come from. We, on the other hand, may take a slightly different approach. Here are a few examples of conversations and questions that have come up in other households with gay dads. Hopefully, they will provide a few ideas for how to have these types of conversations if or when they ever come up in your household.

How Your Family Was Created

"We had to explain the process of surrogacy to our children so they can respond to people with facts when asked if they were adopted or if their mother died."
—**Tommy Starling**

"We have open discussions about anything and everything with our daughter. It is very important to us that she understands she is adopted. She recognizes her biological parents from a photo. She knows them by name and talks about them often."
—**Trey Darnell**

"Our older daughter asked how she and her sister were conceived, which is a question that even the children of straight parents might ask. In our case, we began a co-parenting journey with two lesbians via the proverbial

turkey baster method. One of us dads provided the sperm and handed it off to one of the moms via a plastic syringe. After explaining this and also revealing which of us are their biological parents, our daughter had the follow up question of why was it those two who "made them" (her words), and not the other two parents? I doubt most straight parents have to field that one."
—**Bill Delaney**

Family Structures and Diversity

"We talk about what family means in a pretty expansive way. We talk about adoption, about biological family, and the different ways we inherit traditions, ethnicity, faith, etc. We talk about permanence and how it's OK to have complicated feelings about family, but that no matter what, this family is not going anywhere."
—**Gabriel Blau**

"We have had a lot of conversations about diversity in general, whether it's about them being Latino or having gay dads. We are both Christian, so we try to pass on those values of love, respect, and kindness to our children. We explain to our kids that they should respect people no matter what their beliefs are and they should be open to differing opinions and ideas. Sometimes people don't share our views and they may say or do hurtful things, but that's probably because they don't understand."
—**Jay Foxworthy**

"'Why do I have two daddies and where is my mommy?' We told our son, who is six, that there are families who have one dad and one mom, two mommies or two daddies, or one mom or dad."
—**Mike Degala**

"When our son was younger, we talked at great length about what makes up a family. He had another girl in his class that had two moms, one boy lived with his grandparents, and another spent part of the week with his mom and part of the week with his dad, as they were divorced. This gave us ample opportunity to explain to our son that families come in all different sizes and shapes and that it basically boils down to, 'Your family is whoever loves you and takes care of you!'"
—Del Hubers

"I think the special talks we have with our kids, especially in preparation for going to school, is the idea that their family is different, but that just being different is not a bad thing. We tell them that most kids have a mom and a dad. They don't have a mom, but they have two dads. We say it plainly without implying that anything is missing. It turns out that many of their classmates have parents that are divorced or otherwise split, so they are being raised by a single parent. There isn't necessarily anyone missing from those homes either."
—David Hu

"Our conversations really have been focused around inclusion. We talk about how we are different, but so is every other family. Our kids go to school with children in single-parent homes or a parent in jail. We make sure to explain that common social constructs like the nuclear family are not always common. We also talk about how being different is good. That we bring something special to the table that no one else can. And that everyone, no matter who they are or what they look like, contributes. Sometimes you may have to look for that contribution, but it is always there."
—Duke Nelson

"While we do not focus on our family being different than other families, we do talk about how families can be made in different ways. Being different is interesting and wonderful. We love how inquisitive a toddler can be and we try to capture those moments and turn them into an opportunity for learning. When we embrace being different and thrive in it, we become better dads and better people. If every family or person was the same, that would be pretty boring. We are not boring people unless we are binge watching a television show."
—**Trey Darnell**

Coming Out to Your Kids

"I grew up in the 70s and 80s when being gay was still kind of taboo. Even though I knew I was gay from an early age, I married a woman because I was afraid of being outed and didn't want to upset my parents. The marriage lasted many years and resulted in two children. I have now been married to my husband for ten years and he accepted me, the children, and my 'ex-wife' from the day I met him. When I finally came out to my son, he wanted to know why I had hidden my sexuality for so long and why I had married his mother. He went through a real rough patch of self-harming not long after I and my husband first met and got a flat together and my son needed medical help—it was a late response to my coming out and having a male partner. My husband has had chats with the kids regarding my love for them and my love for my husband. He has told them that I am still their father, despite the fact that I am gay and have a husband."
—**Martyn Floyd**

"My kids didn't know I was gay when they came to live with me after being in the foster care system. I eventually

came out to them a few months later. My oldest didn't believe me right away. 'No, you're not gay,' he said. 'Yes, I am,' I told him. Later that day, he came over to me and said, 'Dad, it's okay. I don't care if you're gay...but I just want you to know, I like girls.'"
—**David Aguirre**

Bullying and Violence

"The topic of the Pulse nightclub shooting came up at school in the aftermath of the tragedy. When my daughter came home from school that day, she told me that she found it really upsetting because I was gay and I could have been there. (She was only eleven years old at the time and didn't understand the distance between Florida and Canada, which is where we live.) She went on to ask why someone would do something so hateful. I told her that not everyone in the world is as accepting as we are, and in some places, people are taught to hate anything that is different from themselves. Sometimes people with hate in their heart do terrible things. I went on to say that we are very lucky to live where we do, and at a time when people are more accepting of other people who are not like them. Not long after, I got a T-shirt in memory of the victims of the Pulse shooting. My daughter liked the shirt and wants me to wear it the next time we go to Pride in Montreal."
—**Peter Leonard**

"I'm always thinking, how do I arm my kid with knowledge? We've talked about diversity like different races and religions. We've talked about not using the word 'gay' as 'lame,' and I've asked my son if he has ever heard the word 'fag' at school. We're pretty lucky though,

because we live in a bubble and his school is LGBT friendly."
—**Frank Lowe**

"We have had several conversations with our children that we know straight parents do not usually have with their children. We have prepared our children for the possibility of being bullied about who their parents are and how to respond. We tell them to be honest and unapologetic about having two gay dads. We tell them to be factual and stern in their response and consult with a teacher if the bullying continues."
—**Tommy Starling**

Discrimination, Anti-LGBT Laws, and Equality

"Our son is in middle school and we try to be proactive but not alarmist. In general terms, we share anything in the news that has (or could have) significant impact on gay families. We'd rather he heard it from us than at school. During the 2016 Presidential election, we had conversations with him about the backlash against the 2015 Freedom To Marry Act and that some people are uncomfortable with Marriage Equality and gay families. We tried to explain why they felt that way and shared that same-sex marriage is a new concept. We explained that attitudes are often slow to change and that some people have difficulty accepting those who are different in their eyes. We tried to prepare him for hearing negative comments about this at school, but he has not reported anything like that to us yet."
—**Michael Hadley**

"The hurtful conversations include explanations about laws that have discriminated against us. Our children do not understand why everyone is not treated equally."
—Tommy Starling

"We live in a conservative town. One day my kids came home from school with Trump stickers and they were excited about the election. I had to sit them down and explain that his beliefs on LGBT equality, women's rights, immigration, basically his whole platform didn't really agree with our lifestyle. The next day they went to school proudly telling everyone they were supporting Hillary Clinton."
—David Aguirre

"Social justice is discussed with our kids in broad terms. We try to demonstrate the importance of sharing and donations, of good manners, kindness, inclusiveness, and civility, and for expressing gratitude. Being in liberal San Francisco, we can't compete with some families in the expression of social outrage, but personally, I'm in no rush to delve into the subject of homophobia. It will come with time. Our kids will know that their dads grew up in a time that people were not very nice for no good reason, but that things are better and more people are more enlightened, and that if they need any proof of that they need only look at our family and friends. But that it's also our responsibility to help make it better for people who may live somewhere less accepting, or in a situation less fortunate than our own…and then we'll have a dance party in the kitchen."
—Ian Hart

Sexuality, Orientation, and the Birds and the Bees

"I think in most families, kids are presumed straight unless told otherwise. I never set an expectation on my kid's identities. That was the case when we eventually had the 'birds and the bees' talk. When I did research to see how other people had the talk with their children, I noticed that it often came up in families because someone got pregnant. The parents would start talking about the mother and father sex part and how a baby is made. I took a different approach and focused the conversation on what intimacy and bonding are. What is sexuality and what is sex? The whole conversation came up because one of my sons came to me and said his brother was misusing the 'F' word and saying it meant sex. I asked if he knew what sex was, and he said no—so we dove into the conversation and they got the whole scope of it. We talked about intimacy, what men's bodies do, and what female bodies do. I explained what happens when men do it, and what happens when women do it. We covered responsibility and sexually transmitted diseases, but the conversation started with intimacy."

—Rob Watson

"My parents never talked to me about sex, and I was sexually active very young. We've been very open with my kids about sex. They understand it can be a good thing or a dangerous thing. We stressed the importance of being protective of themselves and other people. For me, it's all about being open and honest with my kids, and creating an environment where they feel like they can come to us about anything. We have a rule in our house that if our kids do something wrong or bad but come to us and own up to it, there are no consequences. If we find out they

tried to cover something up or lie about it, there will be consequences. My son tried marijuana once and came to tell me about it. That was it. So far it's worked for us."
—Jay Foxworthy

TIP:
If you're looking for a way to talk about reproduction with your kids, check out the book What Makes A Baby, by Cory Silverberg. It's targeted towards readers aged three to seven and covers conception, gestation, and birth in a way that is inclusive of all kinds of kids, adults, and families, regardless of how many people were involved, their orientation, gender identity, or family composition.

Gay Dads Raising
Girls

As a gay man, there is a high probability that there may be a few feminine issues that you haven't had to encounter. So, if you happen to be raising a daughter, what do you do when she hits puberty? How do you know what kind of bra your daughter should wear? Should she be using tampons or pads? Here are a few basics you should know.

When Will My Daughter Start Puberty?

Children go through puberty at various different times. Most girls will start puberty sometime between eight and thirteen years old, but some can start earlier or later. The process normally lasts a few years and starts with the growth of breasts and pubic hair. A little later, hair will begin to grow under her arms and within 1–2½ years after breast development starts, most girls will get their first menstrual period. Every girl is different though, and not all of them follow this development pattern. If signs of puberty start before she is eight years old, or haven't started after thirteen years of age, your daughter should see their pediatrician to rule out potential medical concerns. You can also consult her doctor if you have any other concerns about the timing of her development.

To make puberty easier on your daughter, try to make sure she knows what's going to happen before it starts. If you're uncomfortable having the talk with her, there are plenty of age-appropriate books out there, and because young people tend to be savvy on the Internet, YouTube videos might even work better. There are tons of videos where people explain what it was like when they had their first period or when they went shopping for their first bra. Seeing someone else her age going through the experience and sharing their story may help your daughter relate.

REAL-LIFE STORY:

"As a gay dad, I had concerns about our daughter becoming a young lady, and we weren't sure if we would be able to help her through puberty. How would we talk to her about her period and would she be comfortable hearing these conversations from a man? We talked about the topic early on and even showed her videos online. When the time finally came, she had already been educated. She told us when she spotted so we could take her to the store, and she was very mature about it. There was no fear about coming to us about it, and, for me, that was one of my proudest parenting moments." –Jay Foxworthy

---

What Do I Do When My Daughter Is Ready for Her First Bra?

When it's time to go bra shopping for the first time, consider asking your daughter with whom she wants to go. It could be you or your partner, or maybe she would rather go with a female instead. If that's the case, you may want to ask (or maybe have her ask, if she's more comfortable doing so) someone she feels comfortable being around. This could be her grandmother, aunt, surrogate, birthmother, egg donor, or maybe even her best friend. If she wants you to go with her, here are a few tips to help you get through the experience:

- Discuss the shopping trip beforehand and set a few expectations to make sure you're on the same page. Does she want you with her, or would she rather have you wait nearby? How many will she be buying?

- Bralette, boning, compression bra, convertible, molded, racerback. Understanding bras is like learning a whole new language! Search online for "bra terminology" before you to the store, so you understand the different types of bras and can get a better idea for what you're looking for.

- Determine how you will get the proper size. You can easily find sizing charts online if you want to measure at home, but doing it for the first time might be confusing. A salesperson at the store can measure and help your daughter get the proper fit. If you wind up asking a salesperson for assistance, do so quietly so that you don't embarrass your daughter.

- That brings us to the next point. You know your daughter best, and you may want to crack jokes with her, which is fine, but try not to do anything that will embarrass her during this vulnerable time. It's a big moment for your daughter, but it can also be awkward for her too. The last thing you want to do is make her feel uncomfortable or embarrassed about her body.

- Let her choose the style. This is a big moment for her, so let her pick a color and style that she likes. If you want to set a few guidelines, like nothing that looks like stripper underwear, that's up to you, but don't make her buy something she's uncomfortable with either.

Don't offer to help more than once. If she says she's fine on her own, give her space.

- Once she's selected a few bras, encourage her to try them on in the dressing room. Bras are intended to be worn for support and it's important she gets ones that fit her properly. Getting the wrong size can make her extremely uncomfortable.

- When you find bras that fit your daughter and are comfortable for her to wear, take note of the size, style, and brand name. That way you can order more online when necessary and save yourself a trip back to the underwear section. Her bra size is going to change as she gets older though, so make sure you always get the correct size before buying more.

TIP:
Don't put bras in the dryer, unless you have an air dry or delicate mode available. The heat from the dryer can melt the plastic underwire in bras and cause them to snap in odd places so the wiring pokes the skin. Air-drying is best, but if you need to put them in the dryer, make sure it's on the lowest heat setting, and take them out as soon as they are dry. Alternatively, you could also try to get bras with metal underwire instead of plastic.

How Do I Know Which Pads or Tampons to Get?

When your daughter gets to the point in her life where she's about to get her first period, she's going to need sanitary supplies, but how do you know what to get her?

Many girls start with pads (also called sanitary pads or sanitary napkins), which are rectangular pieces of absorbent material that go inside the underwear. Some have "wings" on the side that fold over the underwear to keep them in place. Other girls may want to use tampons, which are cylinders of absorbent material that are placed inside the vagina; these are especially suited for swimming, or for girls who are active in sports. Some tampons are inserted with a person's fingers, while others have applicators.

Both tampons and pads come in a variety of sizes, for heavier or lighter periods. Don't assume the most absorbent ones are better for every situation. It's possible that super-absorbent pads may wind up looking and even feeling like a diaper, and tampons that are too absorbent can cause discomfort or even gynecological problems. It's best to get the least-absorbent ones she needs. Some pads and tampons even come deodorized, but the scented ones can sometimes irritate the vagina, so you might want to skip those. Try getting a few different brands and types of pads/tampons so your daughter can determine what works best for her.

Also, make sure she knows how often to change them. The frequency will depend on how much blood she has, but it's a good idea to change pads at least every three or four hours even if she's not menstruating much. Tampons should be changed every four to six hours, or when they're saturated with blood. When one is left in too long, bacteria can grow inside it, enter the body from inside the vagina, and then enter the bloodstream. This can put girls at risk for toxic shock syndrome (TSS), a rare but very dangerous illness that can cause high fever, vomiting, diarrhea, muscle aches, dizziness, and/or rashes. Again, it's rare, but the illness can be severe and occasionally life-threatening, so make sure your daughter is aware of TSS and knows that she should remove the tampon and tell an adult immediately if she has any of these symptoms while using one.

Last, but not least, make sure your daughter knows that pads and tampons (even ones that say they're flushable) should not be flushed down the toilet. They should be wrapped in toilet paper and put in a trashcan. If you have dogs or cats at home, make sure the trashcan has a lid on it so that the animals don't get at them.

Tracking Menstrual Cycles

Pregnancy concerns are not the only reason for keeping track of menstrual cycles. Changes in menstrual cycles can also be a sign of a variety of different health issues, including thyroid problems, liver function problems, and diabetes. Irregular periods can also be a result of new exercise routines, gaining or losing a significant amount of weight, or extreme stress. While one late or irregular period isn't necessarily problematic, if it's prolonged or combined with other symptoms, your daughter should consult with a gynecologist or OB/GYN. Keep in mind, though, that it may take a year or more after the onset of menstruation for a young girl to develop regular monthly menstrual cycles that occur for the same number of days.

Every girl should maintain a menstrual calendar to keep track of her periods. It's as simple as marking the start and end date on a calendar. There are also apps for that so it's easy to track anywhere at any time.

How Can I Make Sure My Children Have Strong Female Role Models?

While our children have us as male role models, it's also important that they have strong female role models in their lives to understand that people can do anything, regardless of gender. Role models can be anyone from grandmothers, aunts, and cousins, to birthmothers, egg donors, and surrogates if you have good relationships with them. Teachers, coaches, and group leaders can also be possibilities.

In addition to real-life examples, we can go out of our way to make sure our children are exposed to strong female characters in literature, games, television, and movies. Do an inventory of books, movies, and games in your house every so often and see if there's a balance of gender in them. If not, consider getting a few new items to help offset it. If you need a few ideas for inspiration, A Mighty Girl is a great website that features a collection of books, toys, and movies for smart, confident, and courageous girls. The website can be found at www.amightygirl.com.

LGBT-Friendly Books for Your Kids

There are not many options when it comes to LGBT children's books, but as time goes by, more and more titles are becoming available. While this is not a complete list, here are a few books you might want to consider adding to your personal library. Also, I'm a big believer of: "If you can't find what you're looking for, write it yourself!" We need more books that represent our diverse families, and I'm sure you have a great story to tell.

The Family Book (By Todd Parr) – Written by New York Times bestselling author Todd Parr, this book uses colorful illustrations to show the various different ways that families are unique. Ages 2–5.

Families, Families, Families! (By Suzanne Lang) – This book features various types of family combinations, including same-sex parents and non-traditional family structures. It stresses the message that love makes a family. Ages 3–7.

The Christmas Truck (Authored by J. B. Blankenship; Illustrated by Cassandre Bolan) – This rhyming story tells of a child who works with Papa, Dad, and Grandmother to save Christmas for another kid they never met. Ages 4–8.

What Makes A Baby (Authored by Cory Silverberg; Illustrated by Fiona Smyth) – This picture book covers conception, gestation, and birth and does it in a way that is inclusive of all kinds of kids, adults, and families, regardless of how many people were involved, their orientation, gender identity, or family composition. Ages 3–7.

The Bravest Knight Who Ever Lived (Authored by Daniel Errico; Illustrated by Ida M. Schouw Andreasen) – A young pumpkin farmer goes on a quest to rescue a prince and princess from a fire-breathing dragon, and when the journey ends, he decides whose affectation he truly desires. Ages 4–8.

Rosaline (Authored by Daniel Errico; Illustrated by Michael Scanlon) – A modern take on fairytales that incorporates LGBT themes. A young girl named Rosaline must get past a tricky witch, a hungry wolf, and a bubbly fairy godmother before making it back home to her one true love. Ages 4–8.

Red: A Crayon's Story (By Michael Hall) – A story about a blue crayon wrapped in a red label, this book helps children understand the differences between how someone is on the inside vs. how they are labeled on the outside. Ages 4–8.

ABC: A Family Alphabet Book (Authored by Bobbie Combs; Illustrated by Desiree & Brian Rappa) – This book celebrates LGBT families while teaching the alphabet. Ages 3–5.

King & King (By Linda de Haan and Stern Nijland) – Turning the common fairy tale on its head, King & King tells the story of a prince who is being forced to marry, but he has no interest in marrying a princess. Ages 4–8.

Stella Brings the Family (Authored by Miriam B. Schiffer; Illustrated by Holly Clifton-Brown) – Stella has two dads and isn't sure what to do when her class has a Mother's Day celebration. She winds up bringing her whole family to the party. Ages 4–7.

10,000 Dresses (Authored by Marcus Ewert; Illustrated by Rex Ray) – Baily's parents tell him he shouldn't be thinking about dresses because he's a boy, but after meeting an older girl who is touched by his imagination and courage, the two of them begin making dresses together. Ages 5–9.

In Our Mother's House (By Patricia Polacco) – Marmee, Meema, and the kids are just like any other family on the block, but some of the other families don't accept them because they have two moms and no dad. Marmee and Meema teach their children what it means to be a family. Ages 6–8.

The Purim Superhero (Authored by Elisabeth Kushner; Illustrated by Mike Byrne) – A boy wants to wear an alien costume for Purim, but all of his friends are dressing up as superheroes. His two dads help him come up with a solution. Ages 4–8.

I Am Jazz (Authored by Jessica Herthel and Jazz Jennings; Illustrated by Shelagh McNicholas) – Based on the real-life experience of television personality and LGBTQ rights activist Jazz Jennings, this story details how Jazz and her family realized she was transgender at an early age. Ages 4–8.

Two Dads: A Book About Adoption (Authored by Carolyn Robertson; Illustrated by Sophie Humphreys) – A story about having two dads from the perspective of their son. Ages 4–8.

And Tango Makes Three (Authored by Justin Richardson and Peter Parnell; Illustrated by Henry Cole) – This book is based on a true story about two male penguins who created their own family with the help of a zookeeper. Together, the penguins take care of an egg and raise a baby penguin. Ages 4–8.

Daddy, Papa, and Me (Authored by Lesléa Newman; Illustrated by Carol Thompson) – This durable board book has rhyming text that shows toddlers what it's like to spend time with two fathers. Ages 0–3.

Mommy, Mama, and Me (Authored by Lesléa Newman; Illustrated by Carol Thompson) – This durable board book has rhyming text that shows toddlers what it's like to spend time with two mothers. Ages 0–3.

My Princess Boy (Authored by Cheryl Kilodavis; Illustrated by Suzanne DeSimone) – This book is inspired by the author's son who loves pink, sparkly things and sometimes even wears dresses and tiaras. Ages 4–8.

My Uncle's Wedding (Authored by Eric Ross; Illustrated by Tracy K. Greene) – Full disclosure: I actually wrote this book before I got married and changed my name. During the fight for marriage equality in the US, I got tired of people using children as pawns and saying marriage equality would hurt children, so I decided to do a picture book about a same-sex marriage from the perspective of a child. No struggles or hurdles—just an ordinary marriage like any other. Ages 3–7.

Promised Land (Authored by Adam Reynolds and Chaz Harris; Illustrated by Christine Luiten and Bo Moore) – A fairytale where a prince falls in love with a farm boy, but when the queen remarries, her new husband seeks control of the land the farm boy's family is responsible for protecting. Ages 4–8.

Zak's Safari: A Story About Donor-Conceived Kids of Two-Mom Families (Authored by Christy Tyner; Illustrated by Ciaee) – A boy explains how he was conceived using simple and accurate language. He covers sperm and egg cells, known-donors, donors from sperm banks, and genes. Ages 3–6.

The Princes and the Treasure (Authored by Jeffrey A. Miles; Illustrated by J. L. Phillips) – Two princes go on a quest to find "the greatest treasure in the land" so one of them can save and marry the princess; however, they soon realize "the greatest treasure in the land" is not what they expected. Ages 4–8.

Jacob's New Dress (Authored by Sarah Hoffman and Ian Hoffman; Illustrated by Chris Case) – Jacob wants to wear a dress, but some of the kids at school say he can't wear "girl" clothes. So what does he do? Ages 4–8.

Introducing Teddy: A Gentle Story About Gender and Friendship (Authored by Jess Walton; Illustrated by Dougal MacPherson) – A boy supports his teddy bear's transition from Thomas to Tilly. This is a story about being true to yourself and being a good friend. Ages 3–6.

Donovan's Big Day (Authored by Lesléa Newman; Illustrated by Mike Dutton) – Donovan is excited to be the ring bearer when his two moms get married. Ages 3–7.

Heather Has Two Mommies (Authored by Lesléa Newman; Illustrated by Laura Cornell) – Someone at school asks Heather about her daddy, but Heather doesn't have a dad; she has two moms. When the teacher has the children draw pictures of their families, the kids learn that all families are different. Ages 3–7.

A Peacock Among Pigeons (Authored by Tyler Curry; Illustrated by Clarione Gutierrez) – A colorful peacock finds himself growing up in a flock of grey pigeons, and winds up learning how to stand out when he can't fit in. Ages 4–8.

Worm Loves Worm (Authored by J. J. Austrain; Illustrated by Mike Curato) – When two worms fall in love and plan to get married, their friends want to know who will wear the tux and who will wear the dress. They soon find out, it doesn't matter. Ages 4–8.

This Day in June (Authored by Gayle E. Pitman; Illustrated by Kristyna Litten) – This rhyming book details what you will see at a Pride parade, from families, politicians, and equal rights organizations, to drag queens, shirtless dancers, and people dressed in leather. The main theme is one of inclusivity and the end of the book includes parental tips for discussing gender and sexuality. Ages 4–8.

The Boy Who Cried Fabulous (Authored by Lesléa Newman; Illustrated by Peter Ferguson) – A boy loves calling everything Fabulous, so what happens when his parents ban that word? Ages 3–7.

Emma and Meesha My Boy: A Two Mom Story (Authored by Kaitlyn Considine; Illustrated by Binny Hobbs) – A girl with two moms has to learn how to play nicely with her cat. Ages 3–6.

William's Doll (Authored by Charlotte Zolotow; Illustrated by William Pène du Bois) – William gets teased for wanting a doll, until someone understands that the doll will help him learn to be a loving parent someday. Ages 4–8.

Square Zair Pair (Authored by Jase Peeples; Illustrated by Christine Knopp) – Zairs are creatures that do everything in pairs, one round with one square. One day, two Zairs of the same shape pair for the first time and are rejected by their peers, until they realize different pairs of Zairs make their village stronger. Ages 4–8.

Adopting Our Two Dads: A Story About the Leffew Family (By Luca Panzini) – Based on a true story, this book shows how the Leffews formed their family through adoption. Ages 4–8.

Sex is a Funny Word: A Book About Bodies, Feelings, and You (Authored by Cory Silverberg; Illustrated by Fiona

Smyth) – This is a follow-up to the book What Makes a Baby. It covers bodies, gender, and sexuality in a gender-neutral way. It also includes children and families of all makeups, orientations, and gender identities. Ages 7–10.

Being Jazz: My Life as a (Transgender) Teen (By Jazz Jennings) – This memoir covers what it was like for Jazz Jennings to grow up as a transgender teen. Ages 12–18.

Gay & Lesbian History for Kids: The Century-Long Struggle for LGBT Rights, with 21 Activities (By Jerome Pohlen) – This book covers LGBT history for children. Ages 9 and up.

Resources

Family Organizations

Family Equality Council – National organization that has connected, supported, and represented LGBTQ parents and their children for over thirty years.
http://www.familyequality.org

Modern Family Alliance – Celebrates and supports LGBTQ parents, and prospective parents, in the Greater Kansas City area and beyond.
https://modernfamilyalliance.wordpress.com

Our Family Coalition – Provides support, education, and advocacy for LGBTQ families with children in the California Bay Area.
http://www.ourfamily.org

COLAGE – National organization that unites and supports people with LGBTQ parents.
https://www.colage.org

PFLAG – A national organization that provides information, support, tools, and resources for parents, families, and friends of LGBTQ people.
https://www.pflag.org

School Organizations

GLSEN – A national organization focused on creating safe and affirming school environments for all people, regardless of sexual orientation, gender identity, or gender expression.
https://www.glsen.org

HRC's Welcoming Schools Program – Works to create LGBTQ and gender-inclusive elementary schools by

providing lesson plans, books, and tips.
http://www.welcomingschools.org

Queerly Elementary – Provides workshops, professional development, consulting, classroom lessons, book lists, and other resources to help school communities embrace and celebrate LGBTQ diversity.
http://queerlyelementary.com

Southern Poverty Law Center's Teaching Tolerance Program – Works to reduce prejudice, improve intergroup relations, and support equitable school experiences for our nation's children.
http://www.tolerance.org

GSA Network – An organization that connect GSAs with each other to empower and educate their schools and communities.
https://gsanetwork.org

Campus Pride – An educational organization for LGBTQ and ally college students and campus groups.
https://www.campuspride.org

Advocacy Organizations

Human Rights Campaign (HRC) – America's largest LGBT civil rights organization.
http://www.hrc.org

GLAAD - A national organization that works for fair, accurate, and inclusive representation of the LGBTQ community in the media.
https://www.glaad.org

Equality Federation – An organization that works with state-based equality organizations to strengthen our

movement. Find a state-based equality organization near you.
http://www.equalityfederation.org

National Center for Transgender Equality – A national social justice organization devoted to ending discrimination and violence against transgender people.
http://www.transequality.org

National LGBTQ Task Force – Founded in 1973, this organization is the oldest LGBTQ advocacy group in the United States.
http://www.thetaskforce.org

True Colors Fund – An organization that works to end homelessness among LGBTQ youth.
https://truecolorsfund.org

Support Organizations

Center Link – Find an LGBTQ center near you.
https://www.lgbtcenters.org

The Trevor Project – A national organization that provides crisis intervention and suicide prevention services to LGBTQ youth.
http://www.thetrevorproject.org

The Born This Way Foundation – An organization with a focus on empowering youth.
https://bornthisway.foundation

It Gets Better – An organization focused on communicating the message "It gets better" to LGBTQ youth around the world.
http://www.itgetsbetter.org

Legal Organizations

Lambda Legal
https://www.lambdalegal.org

GLBTQ Legal Advocates & Defenders (GLAD)
https://www.glad.org

National Center for Lesbian Rights (NCLR)
http://www.nclrights.org

American Civil Liberties Union (ACLU)
https://www.aclu.org

Southern Poverty Law Center (SPLC)
https://www.splcenter.org

Transgender Law Center
https://transgenderlawcenter.org

Other Organizations

GLMA (previously known as the Gay & Lesbian Medical Association) – An organization dedicated to ensuring equality in healthcare for LGBT individuals and healthcare providers. They also have a directory of LGBT friendly healthcare professionals.
http://www.glma.org

International Association for Child Safety (IAFCS) – A network of child safety professionals and babyproofers.
www.iafcs.org

R Family Vacations – The first travel company to create vacations for LGBT families and their friends.
http://www.rfamilyvacations.com

Human Milk Banking Association of North America (HMBANA) – A professional association that issues voluntary safety guidelines on screening breast milk donors, in addition to collecting, processing, handling, testing, and storing milk.
www.hmbana.org.

Stopbullying.gov – A website that provides information about bullying from various different government agencies and offers ways to prevent and respond to it.
www.stopbullying.gov

National Gay & Lesbian Chamber of Commerce (NGLCC) – An organization that certifies LGBT-owned businesses and works to expand economic opportunities and advancements for LGBT people.
https://nglcc.org

You Can Play – An organization that works to ensure the safety and inclusion of all in sports—including LGBTQ athletes, coaches and fans.
http://www.youcanplayproject.org

Acknowledgments

I want to take this opportunity to give a shout-out to some of the people who helped get this book published.

First and foremost, thank you to my husband Mat, for all the love and support you gave me while I was working on this project. You helped me carve out time to write and you gave me a swift kick in the butt when I needed it.

Mom, thank you for babysitting while I went through my final edits. I couldn't have gotten through crunch time without you!

Kathleen Archambeau, thanks for reconnecting me with an old acquaintance, and jumpstarting this project

Brenda Knight, thank you for your faith, guidance, and mentorship throughout this journey. You've been a great cheerleader. By the way, I have an idea for another survey…

Christopher McKenney, Michelle Lewy, Morgane Leoni, Henryk Jaronowski, Hugo Villabona, Hannah Paulsen, and the rest of the folks at Mango Publishing. You all played a vital role in getting this book out there. Thank you for being such great partners. I'm so happy you were on my team!

Thanks to Olivia Higgins for helping with the LGBT-friendly schools section. You're a wealth of knowledge, and I appreciate you providing feedback on such short notice.

Thanks to Dr. Raymond Cattaneo for helping with the medical sections of this book. Your advice and feedback were invaluable.

Cathy Sakimura, thanks for coming through again with the legal expertise. You and the team at NCLR have always been there for me and I am forever grateful.

Thank you to everyone who shared their stories with me for this book. Adam White, Bill Delaney, BJ Barone, Chad Scanlon, David Aguirre, David Hu, Del Hubers, Duke Nelson, Trey Darnell, Elliott Kronenfeld, Frank Lowe, Gabriel Blau, Ian Hart, Jay Foxworthy, Martyn Floyd, Michael Degala, Michael Hadley, Peter Leonard, Rob Watson, Shawn Moore, and Tommy Starling. By participating in this project, you've helped tons of future gay dads.

Thank you Stan J. Sloan, Ed Harris, Kim Simes, and the rest of the team at the Family Equality Council for your help with this project and the continued support you've given me throughout my writing career. Christina Young, you're my superhero!

Robbie Hyne, thank you for being an awesome coordinator and for making things happen.

Greg Berlanti, I have admired your work for a long time and I am honored that you helped with this project. Thank you for carving out time during the busy pilot season to focus on this book and thank you for all you have done to increase the visibility of LGBTQ people on television.

And finally, I want to thank everyone who read Journey to Same-Sex Parenthood and encouraged me to write a follow-up. You're the reason this book exists.

CPSIA information can be obtained
at www.ICGtesting.com
Printed in the USA
BVOW08s1400011017

496271BV00003B/3/P